Math in Focus

The Singapore Approach

Student Book

3A

Consultant and Author
Dr. Fong Ho Kheong

Authors
Chelvi Ramakrishnan and Michelle Choo

U.S. Consultants
Dr. Richard Bisk, Andy Clark,
and Patsy F. Kanter

Marshall Cavendish
Education

GREAT SOURCE
HOUGHTON MIFFLIN HARCOURT
Supplemental Publishers

© 2009 Marshall Cavendish International (Singapore) Private Limited

Published by Marshall Cavendish Education
An imprint of Marshall Cavendish International (Singapore) Private Limited
A member of Times Publishing Limited

Marshall Cavendish International (Singapore) Private Limited
Times Centre, 1 New Industrial Road
Singapore 536196
Tel: +65 6411 0820
Fax: +65 6266 3677
E-mail: fps@sg.marshallcavendish.com
Website: www.marshallcavendish.com/education

Distributed by
Great Source
A division of Houghton Mifflin Harcourt Publishing Company
181 Ballardvale Street
P.O. Box 7050
Wilmington, MA 01887-7050
Tel: 1-800-289-4490
Website: www.greatsource.com

First published 2009
Reprinted 2010

Math in Focus ™ is a trademark of Times Publishing Limited.

Great Source ® is a registered trademark of Houghton Mifflin Harcourt Publishing Company.

Math in Focus Grade 3 Student Book A
ISBN 978-0-669-01100-5

Printed in United States of America

2 3 4 5 6 7 8   1897   16 15 14 13 12 11 10
4500219884   B C D E

Contents

Numbers to 10,000

Look for **Practice and Problem Solving**

Student Book A and Student Book B	Workbook A and Workbook B
• **Let's Practice!** in every lesson	• **Independent Practice** for every lesson
• Put on Your Thinking Cap! in every chapter	• Put on Your Thinking Cap! in every chapter

Look for **Assessment Opportunities**

Student Book A and Student Book B	Workbook A and Workbook B
• **Quick Check** at the beginning of every chapter to assess chapter readiness • **Guided Practice** after every example or two to assess readiness to continue lesson • **Chapter Review/Test** in every chapter to review or test chapter material	• **Cumulative Reviews** seven times during the year • **Mid-Year and End-of-Year Reviews** to assess test readiness

Mental Math and Estimation

3 Addition up to 10,000

Subtraction up to 10,000

5 Using Bar Models: Addition and Subtraction

Multiplication Tables of 6, 7, 8, and 9

Multiplication

8 Division

Using Bar Models: Multiplication and Division

Welcome to

Math in Focus™

This exciting math program comes to you all the way from the country of Singapore. We are sure you will enjoy learning math with the interesting lessons you'll find in these books.

What makes *Math in Focus*™ different?

▶ **Two books** You don't write in the ____ in this textbook. This book has a matching **Workbook**. When you see the pencil icon , you will write in the **Workbook**.

▶ **Longer lessons** Some lessons may last more than a day, so you can really understand the math.

▶ **Math will make sense** Learn to use bar models to solve word problems with ease.

In this book, look for

Learn	**Guided Practice**	**Let's Practice**	**ON YOUR OWN**
This means you will learn something new.	Your teacher will help you try some sample problems.	You practice what you've learned to solve more problems. You can make sure you really understand.	Now you get to practice with lots of different problems in your own **Workbook**.

Also look forward to *Games, Hands-On Activities, Math Journals, Let's Explore,* and *Put on Your Thinking Cap!*
You will combine logical thinking with math skills and concepts to meet new problem-solving challenges. You will be talking math, thinking math, doing math, and even writing about doing math.

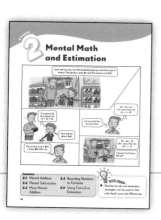

What's in the Workbook?

Math in Focus™ will give you time to learn important new concepts and skills and check your understanding. Then you will use the practice pages in the **Workbook** to try:

▶ Solving different problems to practice the new math concept you are learning. In the textbook, keep an eye open for this symbol **ON YOUR OWN**. That will tell you which pages to use for practice.

▶ *Put on Your Thinking Cap!*

  Challenging Practice problems invite you to think in new ways to solve harder problems.

  Problem Solving challenges you to use different strategies to solve problems.

▶ Math Journal activities ask you to think about thinking, and then write about that!

Students in Singapore have been using this kind of math program for many years.
Now you can too — are you ready?

Chapter 1

Numbers to 10,000

Mount McKinley
in Alaska 6,194 m

Pikes Peak
in Colorado 4,301 m

Mount McKinley is the highest mountain in the United States. It is 6,194 meters high.

Mount Mitchell is the highest peak east of the Mississippi River.

Mount Rainier is higher than Pikes Peak.

Mount Rainier
in Washington 4,392 m

Mount Mitchell
in North Carolina 2,037 m

Lessons

1.1 Counting
1.2 Place Value
1.3 Comparing and Ordering Numbers

BIG IDEA

▶ Count and compare numbers to 10,000.

Recall Prior Knowledge

Counting on

- Count on by ones: 124 125 126 127 128 ...
- Count on by tens: 134 144 154 164 174 ...
- Count on by hundreds: 124 224 324 424 524 ...

Identifying place value

In 937
- the digit 9 is in the hundreds place.
- the digit 3 is in the tens place.
- the digit 7 is in the ones place.
- Standard form: 937
- Word form: nine hundred thirty-seven
- Expanded form: 900 + 30 + 7

Comparing numbers by using a place-value chart

	Hundreds	Tens	Ones
478	4	7	8
678	6	7	8

Compare the hundreds.
400 is less than 600.
So, 478 is less than 678.

Use < to show *less than*.
So, 478 < 678.

678 is greater than 478.
Use > to show *greater than*.
So, 678 > 478.

Using place values to order numbers

Order 385, 198, and 627 from least to greatest.

	Hundreds	Tens	Ones
385	3	8	5
198	1	9	8
627	6	2	7

Compare the hundreds.
627 is greater than 385 and 198.
385 is greater than 198.

So, 627 is the greatest, 198 is the least.

Ordered from least to greatest:

198   385   627
least

Counting on and back to find a pattern

Count on by 10 to find the number that is 10 more.

+10   +10

252   262   272   282   292   302   312

Count back by 100 to find the number that is 100 less.

−100 −100

151   251   351   451   551   651   751   851

✔ Quick Check

Count by ones, tens, or hundreds.

1 206 207 208 ☐ ☐   **2** 614 714 814 ☐ ☐

Express 964 in standard form, word form, and expanded form.

3 standard form ☐

4 word form ☐

5 expanded form ☐

Find the missing number or word.

In the number 327,

6 the digit ☐ is in the hundreds place.

7 the digit 2 is in the ☐ place.

Compare the numbers.

8 Which is greater, 99 or 105? ☐   **9** Which is less, 245 or 708? ☐

Compare. Write < or > .

10 319 ☐ 400   **11** 97 ☐ 164

Find the greatest and least number.
Then order 582, 871, and 339 from greatest to least.

12 ☐ ☐ ☐

Complete each number pattern.

13 842 852 862 ☐ 882 ☐

14 671 571 471 ☐ ☐ 171

Lesson 1.1 Counting

Lesson Objectives

- Use base-ten blocks to count, read, and write numbers to 10,000.
- Count by 1s, 10s, 100s, and 1,000s to 10,000.

Vocabulary
word form

standard form

Learn **Use base-ten blocks to show numbers.**

How many ◼ are there?

There are four hundred twenty-five ◼.

There are 425 ◼.

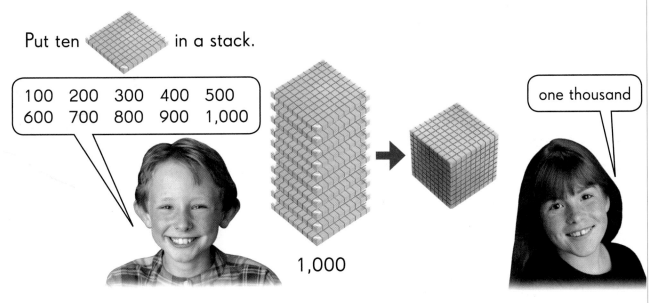

Put ten ▦ in a stack.

100 200 300 400 500
600 700 800 900 1,000

one thousand

1,000

10 hundreds = 1,000

Express a number in different forms.

How many are there?

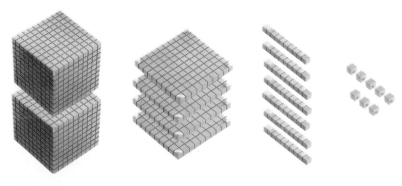

Word form: two thousand, four hundred seventy-eight
Standard form: 2,478

Guided Practice

Look at the base-ten blocks. How many are there?

1. Express in word form.

2. Express in standard form.

Express in word form.

3. 6,257

4. 8,540

5. 7,601

6. 3,094

Express in standard form.

7. eight thousand, six hundred twenty-nine

8. four thousand, seven hundred thirty

9. five thousand, eighty-four

10. seven thousand, ten

Count to ten thousand.

What number comes after 9,999?

10,000
ten thousand

Count on by ones.

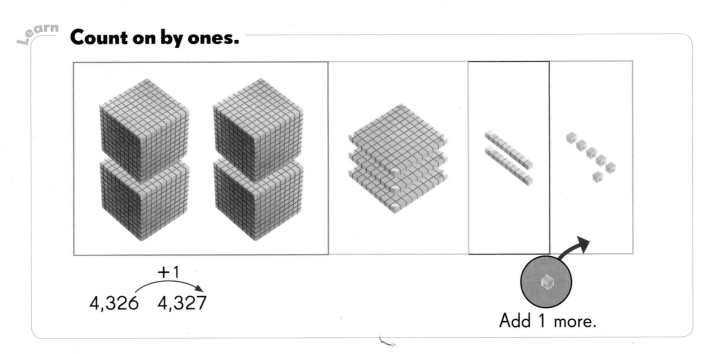

+1

4,326 4,327

Add 1 more.

Guided Practice

**Find each missing number. Count on by ones.
Use base-ten blocks to help you.**

11 1,342 1,343 1,344

12 7,085 7,086 7,087

13 3,497 3,498 3,499

14 9,994 9,995 9,996

Count on by tens.

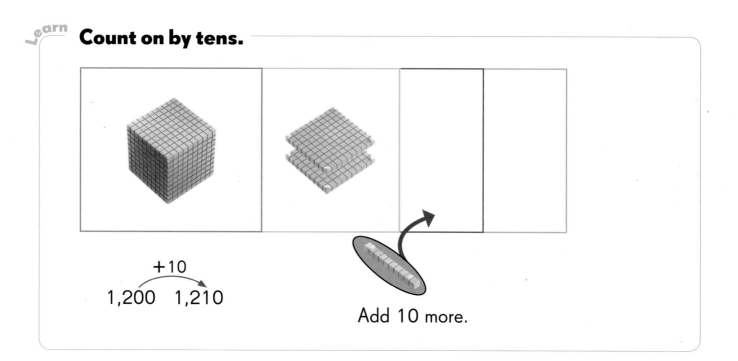

+10

1,200   1,210

Add 10 more.

Guided Practice

Find each missing number. Count on by tens. Use base-ten blocks to help you.

15 3,840   3,850   3,860

16 6,161   6,171   6,181

Count on by hundreds.

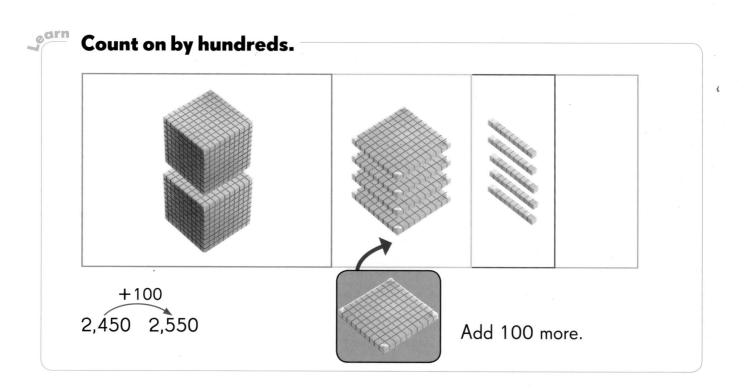

+100

2,450   2,550

Add 100 more.

Find each missing number. Count on by hundreds.
Use base-ten blocks to help you.

17 5,345 5,445 5,545

18 8,670 8,770 8,870

Learn **Count on by thousands.**

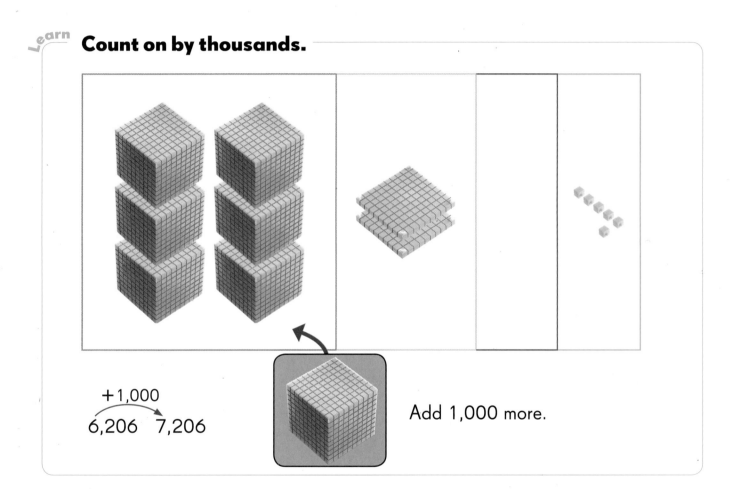

+1,000
6,206 7,206

Add 1,000 more.

Guided Practice

Find each missing number. Count on by thousands.
Use base-ten blocks to help you.

19 4,792 5,792 6,792

20 287 1,287 2,287

21 90 1,090 2,090

Let's Practice

Look at the base-ten blocks.
Express each number in standard form and word form.

1

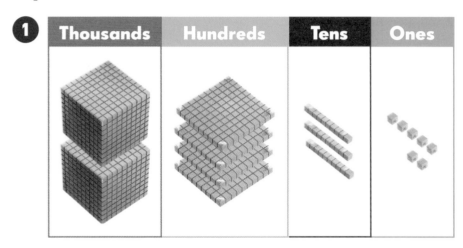

Thousands	Hundreds	Tens	Ones

Standard form:

Word form:

2

Thousands	Hundreds	Tens	Ones

Standard form:

Word form:

Look at the base-ten blocks. Express each number in standard form.

Thousands	Hundreds	Tens	Ones
3			

The chart shows the number ⬚ .

Thousands	Hundreds	Tens	Ones
4			

The chart shows the number ⬚ .

Find each missing number.
Count on by ones, tens, hundreds, or thousands.

5   1,427   1,428   1,429   ⬚   ⬚   ⬚

6   4,356   4,366   4,376   ⬚   ⬚   ⬚

7   7,608   7,708   7,808   ⬚   ⬚   ⬚

8   90   1,090   2,090   ⬚   ⬚   ⬚

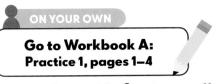

ON YOUR OWN

Go to Workbook A:
Practice 1, pages 1–4

Lesson 1.2 Place Value

Lesson Objectives

- Use base-ten blocks and a place-value chart to read, write, and represent numbers to 10,000.

- Read and write numbers to 10,000 in standard form, expanded form, and word form.

Vocabulary

digit

place-value chart

value

place-value strips

expanded form

Learn Use a place-value chart and place-value strips to find the value of each digit in a number.

How many are there?

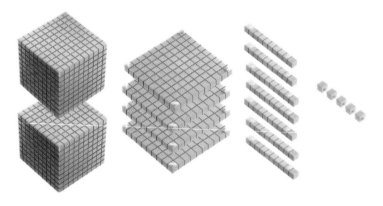

Thousands	Hundreds	Tens	Ones
2	4	7	5

stands for 2 thousands or 2,000

stands for 4 hundreds or 400

stands for 7 tens or 70

stands for 5 ones or 5

This is a **place-value chart**.

In 2,475,
the **digit** 2 is in the thousands place.
the digit 2 stands for 2 thousands or 2,000.
the **value** of the digit 2 is 2,000.

These are **place-value strips**.

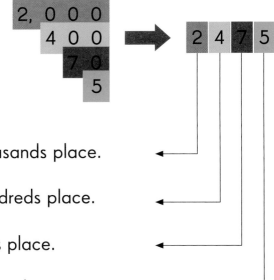

The digit 2 is in the thousands place.

The digit 4 is in the hundreds place.

The digit 7 is in the tens place.

The digit 5 is in the ones place.

2,000, 400, 70, and 5 make 2,475.

The word form of 2,475 is two thousand, four hundred seventy-five.

2,475 = 2 thousands, 4 hundreds 7 tens 5 ones
       = 2,000 + 400 + 70 + 5

2,000 + 400 + 70 + 5 is the **expanded form** of 2,475.

Guided Practice

How many are there? Find the missing numbers.

Thousands	Hundreds	Tens	Ones

1 1,329 = ___ thousand ___ hundreds ___ tens ___ ones

2 1,329 = ___ + ___ + ___ + ___

3 In 1,329,

the digit ___ is in the thousands place.

it stands for ___ .

its value is ___ .

Find each missing number or word.
Use base-ten blocks to help you.

4 In 2,548,

the digit ___ is in the hundreds place.

the digit 4 stands for ___ .

the value of the digit 8 is ___ .

5 In 2,562, the values of the digit 2 are:

2, 5 6 2

___ ⟵⌐   ⌐⟶ ___

Read the place-value strips and complete each sentence.

1,000, 800, 30, and 2 make 1,832.

6　　　　is the standard form of 1,832.

7　　　　is the word form of 1,832.

8　　　　is the expanded form of 1,832.

7,000 and 5 make 7,005.

9　　　　is the standard form of 7,005.

10　　　　is the word form of 7,005.

11　　　　is the expanded form of 7,005.

Roll and Show!

Players: 4 to 8
Materials:
- one 10-sided die
- base-ten blocks
- place-value chart

STEP **1** Form two groups, the Rollies and the Showies.

STEP **2** The Rollies roll the die four times to get four numerals.

STEP **3** The Showies use these numerals to make a 4-digit number. Then they write the number in a place-value chart and show the number using base-ten blocks.

STEP **4** Each group takes turns to roll and show.

The group with the most correct answers wins!

Learn **Use a place-value chart and base-ten blocks to show greater numbers.**

I have 4,827.

Thousands	Hundreds	Tens	Ones

4, 0 0 0
8 0 0
2 0
7

4 thousands 8 hundreds 2 tens 7 ones = 4,827
4,000 + 800 + 20 + 7 = 4,827
4,000, 800, 20, and 7 make 4,827.

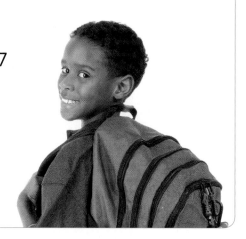

Guided Practice

Find each missing number. Use base-ten blocks to help you.

12 5,000, 300, 10, and 6 make [ ] .

13 7,000, 200, 80, and 9 make [ ] .

14 3,000 + 100 + 70 + 5 = [ ] .

Find each missing word or number.

15 What is the value of each digit?

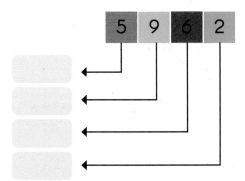

16 In 6,925,

the digit [ ] is in the thousands place.

the digit 9 stands for [ ] .

the value of the digit 2 is [ ] .

Find each missing number.

17 [ ] , 300, 60, and 1 make 4,361.

18 6,720 is 6,000, 700, and [ ] .

Find each missing number.

19 3,000 + 900 + 10 + 5 = [ ] .

20 1,324 = [ ] + 300 + 20 + 4

Let's Practice

Find each missing number.

Thousands	Hundreds	Tens	Ones
3	7	0	0

[blank] thousands [blank] hundreds [blank] tens [blank] ones

The number is [blank].

Express the number formed with the place-value strips in standard form, word form, and expanded form.

2 standard form [blank]

3 word form [blank]

4 expanded form [blank]

```
4, 0 0 0
   8 0 0
     6 0
        5
```

Find each missing number.

5 In 2,839 the digit [blank] is in the thousands place.

6 In 3,571 the digit 5 stands for [blank].

7 In 6,042 the value of the digit 4 is [blank].

Find each missing number.

8 5,000, [blank] , and 5 make 5,805.

9 7,610 = 7,000 + [blank] + 10

10 4,000 + 50 = [blank]

11 8 + 500 + 9,000 = [blank]

ON YOUR OWN

Go to Workbook A:
Practice 2, pages 5–10

Lesson 1.3 Comparing and Ordering Numbers

Lesson Objectives

- Use base-ten blocks to compare and order numbers.

- Use place value to compare and order numbers.

Vocabulary

greater than (>)	greatest
less than (<)	rule
least	number line

Learn Use base-ten blocks to compare and order numbers.

Which is greater, 4,051 or 3,785?

4,051

3,785

Compare the thousands.
4,051 is greater than 3,785.
4,051 > 3,785

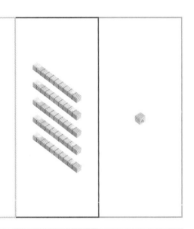

4 thousands is **greater than** 3 thousands.

Guided Practice

Compare the numbers. Choose > or <.

1

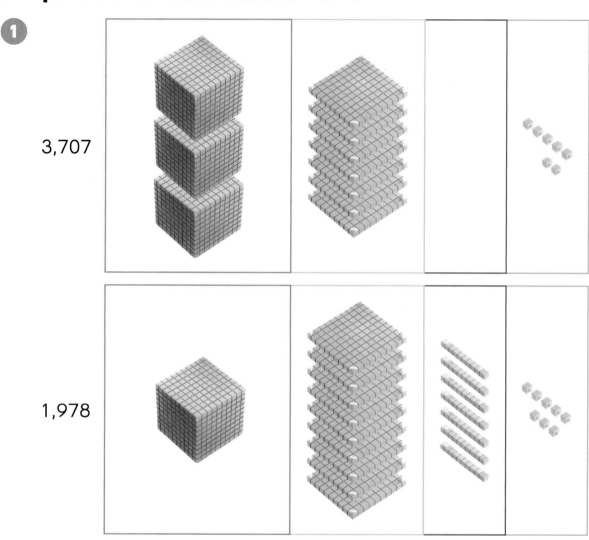

3,707

1,978

3,707 is ⬤ 1,978.

^Learn **Use base-ten blocks to compare and order numbers.**

Which is less, 2,820 or 2,356?

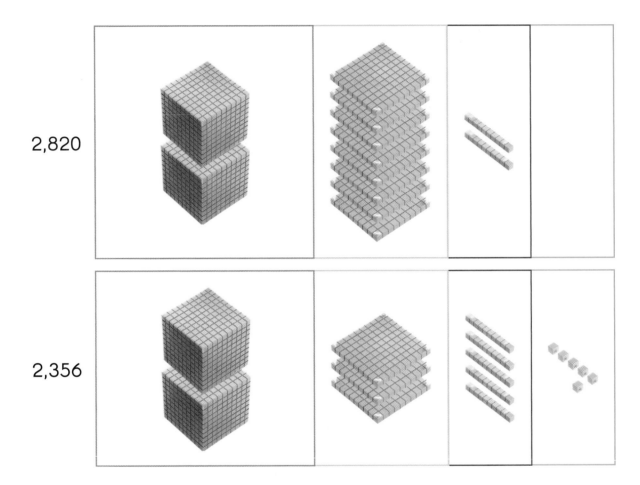

2,820	
2,356	

Step 1 Compare the thousands. They are the same.

Step 2 Compare the hundreds.

3 hundreds is **less than** 8 hundreds.

2,356 is less than 2,820.

2,356 < 2,820

> The two numbers may have the same number of thousands.
> Then you should compare the hundreds.

Guided Practice

Compare the numbers. Choose > or <.

2

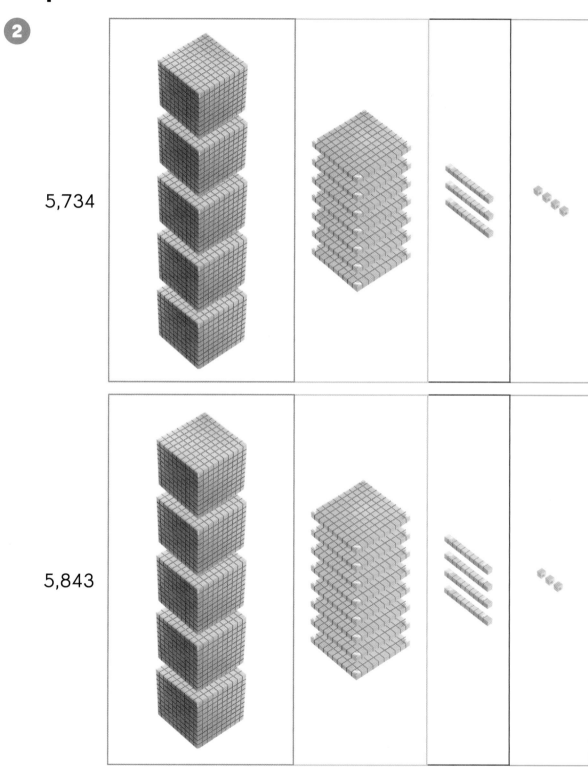

5,734

5,843

5,734 is ⬤ 5,843.

Learn Use place values to compare numbers.

Compare 6,829 and 6,870.

Which is greater?
Which is less?

> The two numbers may have the same number of thousands and hundreds. Then you should compare the tens.

6,870 is greater than 6,829.

6,829 is less than 6,870.

2 tens is less than 7 tens.

Compare 2,748 and 2,745.

Which is greater?

> The two numbers have the same number of thousands, hundreds, and tens. Then you should compare the ones.

2,748 is greater than 2,745.

2,748 > 2,745

8 ones is greater than than 5 ones.

Guided Practice

Compare. Write < or >.

3 4,058 is ⬤ 4,610.

4 6,289 is ⬤ 6,280.

Learn

Using place values to order numbers.

Order 2,389, 3,001, and 3,010 from least to greatest.

	Thousands	Hundreds	Tens	Ones
2,389	2	3	8	9
3,001	3	0	0	1
3,010	3	0	1	0

Compare the thousands.

3,010 and 3,001 are greater than 2,389.
3,010 and 3,001 have the same number of thousands and hundreds.

You should compare the tens.
3,010 is greater than 3,001.

So, 3,010 is the **greatest**.

2,389 is the **least**.

Ordered from least to greatest:

2,389   3,001   3,010
least

Guided Practice

Compare 4,769 4,802, and 4,738.

5 Which is the least?

Which is the greatest?

Order the numbers from greatest to least.

6 4,790 974 7,049 9,107

Hands-On Activity

Players: 2
Materials:
• worksheet

2,314

STEP **1**

Player 1 thinks of a 4-digit number
with 1, 2, 3, and 4.
Use each digit only once.

STEP **2** Player 2 writes his or her first guess in
the first row of the worksheet.

Thousands	Hundreds	Tens	Ones
1	2	4	3

STEP **3**

Player 1 gives some clues.
For example, if Player 1's number is 2,314 and
Player 2's guess is 1,243, Player 1 says:
• My thousands is greater than yours.
• My hundreds is greater than yours.
• My tens is less than yours.
• My ones is greater than yours.

STEP **4** Player 2 writes his or her second
guess in the second row.
If his or her guess is 2,134
Player 1 will say:
• My thousands is the same as yours.
• My hundreds is greater than yours.
• My tens is less than yours.
• My ones is the same as yours.

Thousands	Hundreds	Tens	Ones
1	2	4	3
2	1	3	4

STEP **5**

Thousands	Hundreds	Tens	Ones
1	2	4	3
(2)	1	3	(4)

Player 2 circles the numbers that
are the same as Player 1's.
Player 2 goes on guessing until
he or she gets the correct number.
Switch roles and play again!

Learn Look for patterns on a number line.

Some numbers on the **number line** are missing.
Find the missing numbers.

To find the missing number, look
for a pattern. Its **rule** is to
add 10 to the number before it.

$$+ \, 10$$

1,457   1,467

10 more than
1,457 is 1,467.

1,427   1,437   1,447   1,457   ?   1,477   1,487   ?   1,507   1,517   1,527

10 less than
1,507 is 1,497.

To find the missing number,
the rule for the pattern can
also be to subtract 10 from
the number after it.

$$- \, 10$$

1,497   1,507

Guided Practice

Look for a pattern. Find each missing number.

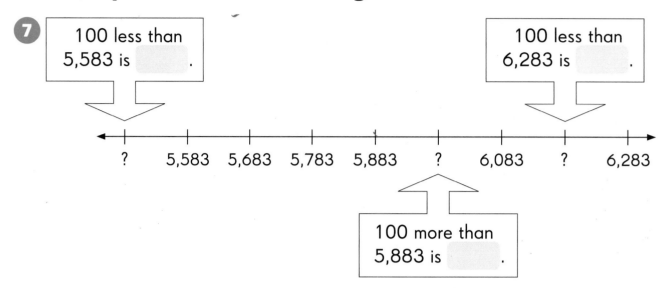

7

100 less than 5,583 is [   ].

100 less than 6,283 is [   ].

100 more than 5,883 is [   ].

Number line: ?   5,583   5,683   5,783   5,883   ?   6,083   ?   6,283

Find each missing number. Use a number line to help you.

8 10 more than 5,893 is [   ].

9 100 less than 3,967 is [   ].

Look for a pattern. Find each missing number.

10

[   ]   1,407   1,417   1,427   [   ]

Complete each number pattern. Use a number line to help you.

11 5,843   5,833   [   ]   5,813   [   ]   [   ]

12 [   ]   [   ]   6,913   [   ]   6,933   6,943

13 7,662   [   ]   7,862   7,962   [   ]   [   ]

14 4,420   4,320   [   ]   4,120   4,020   [   ]

Let's Practice

Compare. Write < or >.

1 999 ⬤ 8,950

2 2,800 ⬤ 2,080

Find each missing number.

3 10 less than 3,415 is ⬜ .

4 100 more than 4,237 is ⬜ .

Look for a pattern. Find each missing number.

5

⬜ 2,415 4,415 ⬜ 8,415

6

1,345 ⬜ 1,945 ⬜ 2,545 2,845

Complete each number pattern. Use a number line to help you.

7 7,200 7,220 7,240 ⬜ 7,280 ⬜ 7,320

8 880 980 ⬜ ⬜ 1,280 1,380 1,480 ⬜ 1,680

9 8,472 8,672 ⬜ ⬜ 9,272 9,472 9,672

ON YOUR OWN

**Go to Workbook A:
Practice 3, pages 11–16**

Use these cards. Make as many numbers as possible with:

1 4 in the thousands place

2 6 in the thousands place

3 How many numbers are there in all?

Subtract the least number from the greatest number in the set of numbers with:

4 4 in the thousands place

5 6 in the thousands place

Math Journal

List the steps to arrange the numbers in order from least to greatest.

Example

> 1,984   2,084   1,884

STEP 1 I compare the thousands.

STEP 2 I can see that 2,084 is the greatest.

STEP 3 I compare the hundreds.

STEP 4 I can see that 1,884 is the least number.

Arranged from least to greatest:

1,884   1,984   2,084
 least

· ·

> 9,049   9,654   8,785

Arranged from least to greatest:

⬜⬜⬜   ⬜⬜⬜   ⬜⬜⬜

List the steps to get your answer.

PROBLEM SOLVING

Rita wrote three 4-digit numbers on a sheet of paper.
She accidentally spilled some ink on the paper.
Some digits were covered by the ink.
Using the clues given, help Rita find the digits covered by the ink.

CLUES

The sum of all the ones is 17.

The ones digit of the first number is the greatest 1-digit number.

The digit in the tens place of the second number is one more than the digit in the tens place of the first number.

The tens digit of the third number is 4 less than the tens digit of the second number.

ON YOUR OWN

Go to Workbook A: Put on Your Thinking Cap! pages 17–18

Chapter Wrap Up

Study Guide
You have learned...

Numbers to 10,000

Read, Write and Count

9,745
- Expanded form:
  9,000 + 700 + 40 + 5
- Word form:
  nine thousand, seven hundred forty-five
- Standard form: 9,745

Count by
- ones: 3,928 3,929 3,930...
- tens : 2,096 2,106 2,116...
- hundreds: 813   913   1,013...
- thousands: 4,126 5,126 6,126...

Compare and Order

| 1,638 | 1,728 | 1,629 | 2,268 |

Order the numbers from greatest to least.

- Compare the thousands.
  2,268 is the greatest number.
- Compare the hundreds.
  1,728 is greater than 1,638 and 1,629.
- Compare the tens.
  1,629 is the least number.
  2,268 1,728 1,638 1,629
  greatest

Place Value

| 9 | 7 | 4 | 5 |

9 thousands ←
7 hundreds ←
4 tens ←
5 ones ←

Patterns

Number Patterns   +10
- 2,304 2,314 2,324 2,334...
          +100
- 3,619 3,719 3,819 3,919...
                  −10
- 5, 811 5,801 5,791 5,781...
          −100
- 7,235 7,135 7,035 6,935...

Chapter Review/Test

Vocabulary
Choose the correct word.

> thousands
> expanded
> rule
> standard

1 The _____ form of 3,614 is 3,000 + 600 + 10 + 4.

2 In a 4-digit whole number, the greatest place value is _____.

3 The _____ form of 2,193 is 2,193.

Concepts and Skills
Express each number in different forms.

4 Express 8,056 in word form. _____

5 Express 6,254 in standard form and expanded form. _____ _____

Complete.
In 1,984,

6 the digit 9 is in the _____ place.

7 the value of the digit 1 is _____.

8 the digit 8 stands for _____.

Compare. Write > or <.

9 3,765 _____ 3,657

10 6,212 _____ 8,523

Identify the least number and the greatest number.

11 3,615   3,156   3,561

Order the numbers from least to greatest.

12 6,028   8,620   960

13 9,143   9,034   9,134

14 3,256   3,279   3,238

15 7,425   7,429   7,420

Find each missing number.

16 1 more than 6,722 is [ ] .

17 10 more than 2,863 is [ ] .

18 100 more than 829 is [ ] .

19 1,000 more than 988 is [ ] .

20 1 less than 3,890 is [ ] .

21 10 less than 8,742 is [ ] .

22 100 less than 526 is [ ] .

23 1,000 less than 4,059 is [ ] .

Complete each number pattern.

24 3,645   3,545   3,445   [ ]   3,245

25 5,014   6,014   [ ]   8,014   9,014

Mental Math and Estimation

Lessons

BIG IDEA

▶ Number bonds and estimation strategies can be used to find and check sums and differences.

Recall Prior Knowledge

Making number bonds

   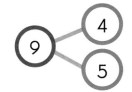

Adding using number bonds

4 + 5 = 9

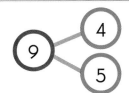

Adding by making 10

7 + 5 = ?

3   2

7 + 3 = 10
10 + 2 = 12

So, 7 + 5 = 12

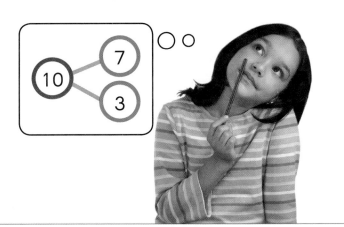

Addition using the 'adding 10, then subtracting the extra ones' strategy

24 + 7 = ?

24 + 10 = 34
34 − 3 = 31

So, 24 + 7 = 31

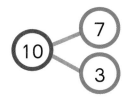

Adding 7 is the same as adding 10, then subtracting 3.

Subtracting using number bonds

8 − 3 = 5

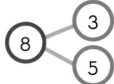

Subtraction using the 'subtracting 10, then adding the extra ones' strategy

35 − 8 = ?

35 − 10 = 25

25 + 2 = 27

So, 35 − 8 = 27

Subtracting 8 is the same as subtracting 10, then adding 2.

Rounding to estimate sums and differences and to check reasonableness of answers

249 + 42 = 291

249 is about 250.

42 is about 40.

250 + 40 = 290

249 + 42 is about 290.

The answer is reasonable.

374 − 58 = 316

374 is about 370.

58 is about 60.

370 − 60 = 310

374 − 58 is about 310.

The answer is reasonable.

Find the missing numbers.

1

2

Find the missing numbers.

3 6 = [ ] + 5

4 2 + [ ] = 10

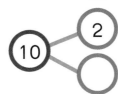

Add by making 10.

5 Find 6 + 9.

9 + [ ] = 10

10 + [ ] = [ ]

So, 6 + 9 = [ ].

Add. Use the 'adding 10, then subtracting the extra ones' strategy.

6 Find 26 + 8.

26 + [ ] = [ ]

[ ] − [ ] = [ ]

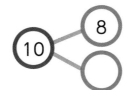

So, 26 + 8 = [ ].

Find the missing numbers.

7 9 − 3 = ⬚

8 5 − ⬚ = 1

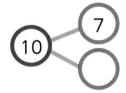

Subtract. Use the 'subtracting 10, then adding the extra ones' strategy.

9 Find 55 − 7.

55 − ⬚ = ⬚

⬚ + ⬚ = ⬚

So, 55 − 7 = ⬚ .

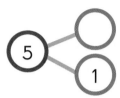

Solve.

10 Find the sum of 319 and 73. Use rounding to check that your answer is reasonable.

11 Find the difference between 825 and 98. Use rounding to check that your answer is reasonable.

Mental Addition

Lesson Objective

- Add 2-digit numbers mentally with or without regrouping.

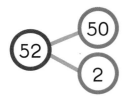

Add 2-digit numbers mentally using the 'add the tens, then add the ones' strategy.

Find 34 + 52.

52 = ⬜ tens ⬜ ones

Step 1 Add 5 tens to 34.   34 + 50 = 84

Step 2 Add 2 ones to the result.   84 + 2 = 86

So, 34 + 52 = 86.

Guided Practice

Add mentally. Use number bonds to help you.

1 Find 45 + 23.

23 = ⬜ tens ⬜ ones

Step 1 Add ⬜ tens to 45.   45 + ⬜ = ⬜

Step 2 Add ⬜ ones to the result.   ⬜ + ⬜ = ⬜

So, 45 + 23 = ⬜.

Learn

Add 2-digit numbers mentally using the 'add the tens, then subtract the extra ones' strategy.

Find 34 + 48.

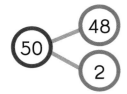

Step 1 Add 50 to 34.   34 + 50 = 84

Step 2 Subtract 2 from the result.   84 − 2 = 82

So, 34 + 48 = 82.

> Do you know why you add 50 and then subtract 2?

Guided Practice

Add mentally. Use number bonds to help you.

2 Find 35 + 57.

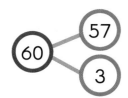

Step 1 Add ⬚ to 35.   35 + ⬚ = ⬚

Step 2 Subtract ⬚ from the result.   ⬚ − ⬚ = ⬚

So, 35 + 57 = ⬚.

Add Mentally!

Players: 2 to 5
Material:
* cards with numbers from 35 to 55

STEP 1 Player 1 says a number from 11 to 44.

STEP 2 Player 1 then draws a card.

STEP 3 Player 1 adds the two numbers mentally and tells the other players his or her answer.

$$20 + 46 = 66$$

STEP 4 The other players check the answer. Player 1 gets 1 point if the answer is correct.

$$66 - 46 = 20$$
$$-20 = 46$$

STEP 5 Return the card to the table and mix them up. Take turns to play three rounds each.

The player with the most points wins!

Let's Practice

Find the missing numbers.

1 38 = 3 tens [ ] ones

2 62 = [ ] tens 2 ones

Add mentally. Use number bonds to help you.

3 Find 11 + 37.

37 = [ ] + [ ]

11 + [ ] = [ ]

[ ] + [ ] = [ ]

So, 11 + 37 = [ ] .

4 Find 66 + 23.

23 = [ ] + [ ]

66 + [ ] = [ ]

[ ] + [ ] = [ ]

So, 66 + 23 = [ ] .

5 25 + 42 = [ ]

6 56 + 32 = [ ]

7 33 + 46 = [ ]

8 41 + 57 = [ ]

Add mentally. Use number bonds to help you.

9 Find 46 + 47.

46 + 50 = [ ]

[ ] − 3 = [ ]

So, 46 + 47 = [ ] .

10 Find 28 + 36.

28 + 40 = [ ]

[ ] − 4 = [ ]

So, 28 + 36 = [ ] .

11 13 + 49 = [ ]

12 24 + 48 = [ ]

13 37 + 56 = [ ]

14 56 + 28 = [ ]

ON YOUR OWN

**Go to Workbook A:
Practice 1, pages 19–20**

Lesson Objective

- Subtract 2-digit numbers mentally with or without regrouping.

Learn **Subtract 2-digit numbers mentally using the 'subtract the tens, then subtract the ones' strategy.**

Find 87 − 34.

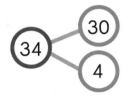

34 = 3 tens 4 ones

Step 1 Subtract 3 tens from 87.   87 − 30 = 57

Step 2 Subtract 4 ones from the result.   57 − 4 = 53

So, 87 − 34 = 53.

Guided Practice

Subtract mentally. Use number bonds to help you.

1 Find 79 − 45.

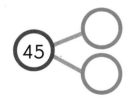

45 = ____ tens ____ ones

Step 1 Subtract ____ tens from 79.   79 − ____ = ____

Step 2 Subtract ____ ones from the result.   ____ − ____ = ____

So, 79 − 45 = ____ .

Learn Subtract 2-digit numbers mentally using the 'subtract the tens, then add the extra ones' strategy.

Find 63 − 48.

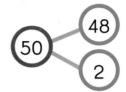

Step 1 Subtract 50 from 63.   63 − 50 = 13

Step 2 Add 2 to the result.   13 + 2 = 15

So, 63 − 48 = 15.

> Do you know why you subtract 50 and then add 2?

Guided Practice

Subtract mentally. Use number bonds to help you.

2 Find 72 − 47.

Step 1 Subtract ____ from 72.   72 − ____ = ____

Step 2 Add ____ to the result.   ____ + ____ = ____

So, 72 − 47 = ____ .

3 96 − 38 = ____

Subtract Mentally

Players: **2 to 5**
Materials:
- cards with numbers from 35 to 55

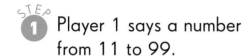

STEP 1 Player 1 says a number from 11 to 99.

80

STEP 2 Player 1 then draws a card.

35

STEP 3 Player 1 mentally subtracts the number that is less from the greater number, and gives the other players his or her answer.

80 − 35 = 45

STEP 4 The other players check the answer. Player 1 gets 1 point if the answer is correct.

45 + 35 = 80

35 + ___ = 80

STEP 5 Return the card to the table and mix the cards up. Take turns to play three rounds each.

The player with the most points wins!

Let's Practice

Find the missing numbers.

1 42 = 40 + [ ]

2 76 = [ ] + 6

Subtract mentally. Use number bonds to help you.

3 Find 77 − 46.

46 = [ ] + [ ]

77 − [ ] = [ ]

[ ] − [ ] = [ ]

So, 77 − 46 = [ ] .

4 Find 66 − 23.

23 = [ ] + [ ]

66 − [ ] = [ ]

[ ] − [ ] = [ ]

So, 66 − 23 = [ ] .

5 49 − 26 = [ ]

6 76 − 42 = [ ]

7 87 − 34 = [ ]

8 98 − 23 = [ ]

Subtract mentally. Use number bonds to help you.

9 Find 65 − 47.

65 − 50 = [ ]

[ ] + [ ] = [ ]

So, 65 − 47 = [ ] .

10 Find 73 − 46.

73 − 50 = [ ]

[ ] + [ ] = [ ]

So, 73 − 46 = [ ] .

11 64 − 38 = [ ]

12 72 − 46 = [ ]

13 82 − 67 = [ ]

14 95 − 29 = [ ]

ON YOUR OWN

**Go to Workbook A:
Practice 2, pages 21–24**

Lesson 2.3 More Mental Addition

Lesson Objective

- Use different strategies to add 2-digit numbers close to 100 mentally.

Learn **Add 2-digit numbers mentally using the 'adding 100, then subtracting the extra ones' strategy.**

Find 86 + 95.

Step 1 Add 100 to 86. 86 + 100 = 186

Step 2 Subtract 5 from 186. 186 − 5 = 181

So, 86 + 95 = 181.

> Do you know why you add 100 and then subtract 5?

Guided Practice

Add mentally. Use number bonds to help you.

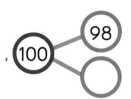 Find 75 + 98.

Step 1 Add 100 to 75.   ⬚ + ⬚ = ⬚

Step 2 Subtract ⬚ from ⬚ .   ⬚ − ⬚ = ⬚

So, 75 + 98 = ⬚ .

Lesson 2.3 More Mental Addition   **49**

Learn Add 2-digit numbers mentally using the 'add the hundreds, then subtract the extra ones' strategy.

Find 94 + 97.

94 and 97 are each near 100.

Subtracting 6 and 3 is the same as subtracting 9.

Step 1 Add the hundreds.
100 + 100 = 200

Step 2 Subtract 6 and 3 from 200.
200 − 6 − 3 = 191

So, 94 + 97 = 191.

Guided Practice

Add mentally. Use number bonds to help you.

2 Find 95 + 99.

95 and 99 are each near 100.

Step 1 Add the hundreds.

100 + 100 = ☐

Step 2 Subtract the ones from ☐ .

☐ − ☐ − ☐ = ☐

So, 95 + 99 = ☐ .

Game

More Mental Addition!

Players: **2** to **5**
Materials:
- a number cube
- cards with numbers 92 to 99

STEP 1 Player 1 rolls the number cube twice to make a 2-digit number.

STEP 2 Player 1 then draws a card.

STEP 3 Player 1 mentally adds the two numbers and tells the other players his or her answer.

$65 + 99 = 164$

STEP 4 The other players check the answer. Player 1 gets 1 point if the answer is correct.

$164 - 99 = 65$

$+65 = 164$

STEP 5 Return the card to the table and mix the cards up. Take turns to play three rounds each.

The player with the most points wins!

Let's Practice

Add mentally. Use number bonds to help you.

1 Find 63 + 99.

63 + 100 = [ ]

[ ] − [ ] = [ ]

So, 63 + 99 = [ ] .

2 Find 47 + 97.

47 + 100 = [ ]

[ ] − [ ] = [ ]

So, 47 + 97 = [ ] .

3 28 + 99 = [ ]

4 38 + 96 = [ ]

5 48 + 95 = [ ]

6 41 + 98 = [ ]

Add mentally. Use number bonds to help you.

7 92 + 96 = [ ]

  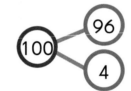

8 98 + 95 = [ ]

9 93 + 99 = [ ]

ON YOUR OWN

Go to Workbook A:
Practice 3, page 25–26

Rounding Numbers to Estimate

Lesson Objective

- Round numbers to estimate sums and differences.

Vocabulary
rounded   reasonable
estimate   overestimate

Round a 3-digit number down to the nearest hundred.

223 beads are in Box A.
The number of beads in Box A is 200 when rounded to the nearest hundred.

223 is between 200 and 300.
It is nearer to 200 than to 300 on the number line.
So, 223 is 200 when **rounded** to the nearest hundred. 223 is about 200.

200 is an **estimate**. It is a number that is close to the exact number.

Round a 3-digit number up to the nearest hundred.

287 beads are in Box B.
The number of beads in Box B is 300 when rounded to the nearest hundred.

287 is between 200 and 300.
It is nearer to 300 than to 200 on the number line.
So, 287 is 300 when rounded to the nearest hundred. 287 is about 300.

Continued on next page

Box C

650

600   700

650 beads are in Box C. The number of beads in Box C is 700 when rounded to the nearest hundred.

650 is exactly halfway between 600 and 700 on the number line. So, 650 is 700 when rounded to the nearest hundred. 650 is about 700.

> **Rounding to the nearest 100.** Look at the digit in the tens place. If it is 1, 2, 3, or 4, round to the hundred that is less. If it is 5, 6, 7, 8, or 9, round to the greater hundred.

Guided Practice

Round each number to the nearest hundred.

1. 216

2. 550

3. 360

4. 950

Round a 4-digit number to the nearest hundred.

Round 2,329 and 2,382 to the nearest hundred.

2,329   2,382

2,300   2,350   2,400

2,329 is between 2,300 and 2,400. It is nearer to 2,300 than to 2,400 on the number line. So, 2,329 is 2,300 when rounded to the nearest hundred. 2,329 is about 2,400.

2,382 is between 2,300 and 2,400. It is nearer to 2,400 than to 2,300 on the number line. So, 2,382 is 2,400 when rounded to the nearest hundred. 2,382 is about 2,400.

Guided Practice

Round 4,632 to the nearest hundred.

5

4,632
↓

4,600 ⟵———————⟶ 4,650 ———————— 4,700

4,632 is between [ ] and [ ] .

4,632 is nearer to [ ] than to [ ] .

4,632 is [ ] when rounded to the nearest hundred.

For each number, draw a number line and mark (X) the number on the number line.
Use the number line to round each number to the nearest hundred and circle it.

Example

Round 8,950 to the nearest hundred.

To decide on where to start and end a number line, look at each number and find the nearest hundred before and after it. In the example, 8,950 is between these two nearest hundreds.

8,900 ⟵ nearest hundred before it   8,950   nearest hundred after it ⟶ 9,000

So, the number line for 8,950 starts at 8,900 and ends at 9,000.

8,900 ——————— 8,950 ——————— (9,000)

8,950 is 9,000 when rounded to the nearest hundred.

6 5,050

7 4,158

8 2,502

9 9,050

Round each number to the nearest ten and hundred.

	Number	Rounded to the Nearest	
		Ten	Hundred
10	68		
11	482		
12	3,209		

Use number lines to help you.

13 List five whole numbers that round to 2,800 when rounded to the nearest hundred.
Use your answers to mark (**X**) the least and the greatest numbers on the number line.

2,700   2,800   2,900

Mark (X) the least and the greatest numbers on the number line that round to 9,300 when rounded to the nearest hundred.

14

9,200   9,300   9,400

Hands-On Activity

Look at the map below. It shows the driving distances between some U.S. cities and Kansas City.

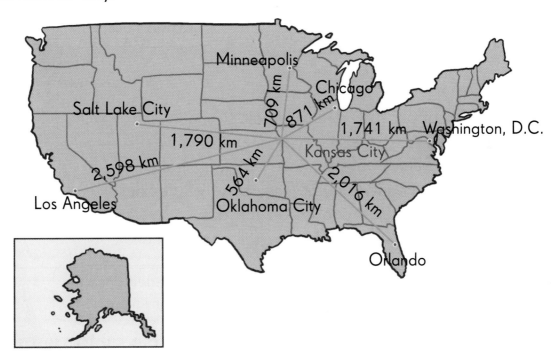

Round each distance to the nearest hundred kilometers.

Example

The distance between Kansas City and Minneapolis is 709 kilometers. 709 kilometers is 700 kilometers when rounded to the nearest hundred kilometers.

Learn Decide whether to find an estimate or an exact amount.

Nita has 178 pennies in her piggy bank.
Eduardo has 231 pennies in his piggy bank.
About how many pennies do they have in all?

Round the number of pennies
each child has to the nearest hundred.

You can estimate
the answer since
the question asks
'**about** how many'.

178 rounds to 200.
231 rounds to 200.

200 + 200 = 400

They have about 400 pennies in all.

. . . .

Some Girl Guides have to make 500 oatmeal
cookies for a charity fun fair. They bake 92 cookies
on Monday and 268 cookies on Tuesday.
How many more cookies do they still have to make?

92 + 268 = 360
500 − 360 = 140

An exact answer is needed since the
question asks 'how many more'.

They still have to make 140 more cookies.

Guided Practice

Decide whether to find an estimate or an exact answer. Solve.

15 Mrs. Thornton is 59 inches tall.
She wears heels that are 3 inches tall.
How tall is Mrs. Thornton with her shoes on?

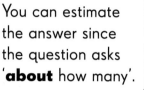

59 in.   ? in.

3 in.

16 A bakery sells 379 muffins on Monday.
It sells 481 muffins on Tuesday.
About how many muffins does it sell on both days?

Learn

Decide whether to find an estimate or an exact amount.

Mrs. Blake has $900. She wants to buy an oven for $257
and a washing machine for $518.
Does Mrs. Blake have enough money?

Do you need an exact answer or an estimate?

You can use an estimate to see if
Mrs. Blake has enough money.

Round each amount of money to the nearest hundred.
257 is 300.
518 is 500.
300 + 500 = 800
Mrs. Blake has enough money.

· ·

Darren has $335.

After buying two of the chairs, Darren has $136 left.

SALE
Dining chair $122
Arm chair $177
Computer chair $138

ⓐ How much do the two chairs cost?

ⓑ Which two chairs does Darren buy?

Do you need an exact answer or an estimate?

ⓐ You need an exact answer since the
question asks **'how much'**.
$335 − $136 = $199
The two chairs cost $199.

ⓑ An estimate is enough to decide which two chairs Darren buys.
Round the cost of each item to the nearest hundred.
Dining chair   122 rounds to 100.
Arm chair   177 rounds to 200.
Computer chair   138 rounds to 100.

$199 is closer to $200 than $300.

$100 + $200 = $300
The dining chair and the arm chair cost about $300.
$100 + $100 = $200
The dining chair and the computer chair cost $200.
So, Darren buys the dining chair and the computer chair.

Guided Practice

Decide whether to find an estimate or an exact answer. Solve.

17 A tennis club orders 715 tennis balls
After some matches, 318 balls are worn out.
The remaining matches will use 415 tennis balls.
Does the club have enough balls for the remaining matches?

18 Maria has 557 beads. She gives 156 beads to her sister.
She wants to use the rest of the beads to make two patterns in her dress.
Pattern A   159 beads
Pattern B   301 beads
Pattern C   242 beads

a   How many beads does she use to make the patterns?

b   Which two patterns can she sew?

19 Renaldo wants to tile his floor.
He has 899 tiles.
172 tiles are damaged.
Bedroom   235 tiles
Living room   523 tiles
Kitchen room   656 tiles

a   How many tiles does he have left to tile his floors?

b   Which two rooms can he tile?

Use rounding to check the reasonableness of sums.

Find 182 + 415.

Then use rounding to check that your answer is reasonable.

182 + 415 = 597

Step 1 Round each number to the nearest hundred.

182 rounds to 200.

415 rounds to 400.

182 is about 200.
415 is about 400.

Step 2 Add the rounded numbers.

200 + 400 = 600

So, 182 + 415 is about 600.

597 is close to 600, so the answer is **reasonable**.

Guided Practice

Find the sum. Then use rounding to check that your answer is reasonable.

20 Find 281 + 532.

281 + 532 = ▢

281 rounded to the nearest hundred is ▢ .

532 rounded to the nearest hundred is ▢ .

▢ + ▢ = ▢

So, 281 + 532 is about ▢ .

Is your answer reasonable?

Find the sum. Then use rounding to check that your answer is reasonable. Round each number to the nearest hundred.

21 434 + 512 = ▢
Is your answer reasonable?

22 818 + 103 = ▢
Is your answer reasonable?

Learn **Use rounding to check the reasonableness of differences.**

Find 588 − 275.

Then use rounding to check that your answer is reasonable.

588 − 275 = 313

Step 1 Round each number to the nearest hundred.

588 rounds to 600.

275 rounds to 300.

Step 2 Subtract the rounded numbers.

588 is about 600.
275 is about 300.

600 − 300 = 300

So, 588 − 275 is about 300.

313 is close to 300, so the answer is reasonable.

Guided Practice

Find the difference. Then use rounding to check that your answer is reasonable. Round each given number to the nearest hundred.

23 Find 677 − 311.

677 − 311 = [ ]

677 rounded to the nearest hundred is [ ].

311 rounded to the nearest hundred is [ ].

[ ] − [ ] = [ ]

So, 677 − 311 is about [ ].

Is your answer reasonable?

24 426 − 296 = [ ]

Is your answer reasonable?

25 852 − 463 = [ ]

Is your answer reasonable?

Let's Practice

**Mark (X) each number on the number line.
Then round each number to the nearest hundred and circle it on the
number line.**

| 500 | 600 | 700 | 800 | 900 | 1,000 |

1 830   **2** 970   **3** 650

**Draw a number line and mark (X) each number on the number line.
Then, round the number to the nearest hundred and circle it on the
number line.**

4 4,283   **5** 3,267   **6** 7,235
4,300   3,300

**Find the sum or difference. Then use rounding to check
that your answer is reasonable.**

7 501 + 286   **8** 478 − 214

9 368 + 495   **10** 827 − 459

Solve. Find the estimate.

11 Mrs. Smith wants to buy a pair of pants that costs $168 and a handbag that costs $535. Estimate the total cost of the two items. Would Mrs. Smith have enough money to buy the two items if she had $600?

12 Tanya has $158 and the cost of a bookshelf is $317. About how much more does she need to buy the bookshelf?

ON YOUR OWN

Go to Workbook A:
Practice 4, page 27–30

Lesson 2.5 Using Front-End Estimation

Lesson Objective
- Use front-end estimation to estimate sums and differences.

Vocabulary
leading digit
front-end estimation

Learn Find the leading digit in a number.

Look at the numbers.

438   **2**,875

The front-end or leading digit for **4**38 is 4.

The front-end or leading digit for **2**,875 is 2.

The **leading digit** in a number is the digit with the greatest place value.

Guided Practice

Name the leading digit in each number.

1. 712

2. 567

3. 309

4. 9,543

5. 2,485

6. 8,021

Complete.

7. Write a 3-digit number where the leading digit is 9.

8. Write a 3-digit number where the leading digit is 5.

9. Write a 4-digit number where the leading digit is 3.

10. Write a 4-digit number where the leading digit is 8.

Use front-end estimation to estimate sums and differences.

Estimate 609 + 395.

609 + 395

↓ ↓

600 + 300 = 900

The leading digit of **6**09 is 6.
The leading digit of **3**95 is 3.

· ·

Estimate 764 − 385.

764 − 385

↓ ↓

700 − 300 = 400

764 **3**85

↑   ↑

Leading digits

Front-end estimation uses leading digits to estimate sums and differences.

Guided Practice

Solve.
Use front-end estimation to help you.

11 Mr. Moore buys 329 paper clips.
Mrs. Moore buys 518 paper clips
Estimate the number of paper clips they have in all.

12 Brendan collects 987 bookmarks.
Casey collects 475 bookmarks.
About how many more bookmarks does Brendan have than Casey?

Use front-end estimation to check reasonableness of sums and differences.

Find 636 + 289.

636 + 289 = 925

636 + 289

$$\downarrow \quad \downarrow$$

600 + 200 = 800

The estimated sum is 800.

So, the answer is reasonable.

The leading digit of **6**36 is 6.
The leading digit of **2**89 is 2.

. . . .

Find 514 − 135.
514 − 135 = 379
514 − 135

$$\downarrow \quad \downarrow$$

500 − 100 = 400
The estimated difference is 400.

So, the answer is reasonable.

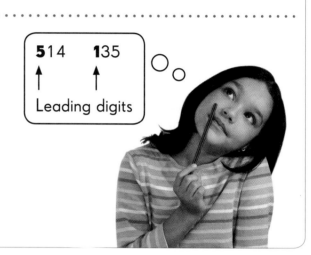

514   **1**35

$$\uparrow \quad \uparrow$$

Leading digits

Guided Practice

Find the sum. Then use front-end estimation to check that your answer is reasonable.

13 Find 520 + 479.

520 + 479 = ⬚

527 + 479

$$\downarrow \quad \downarrow$$

⬚ + ⬚ = ⬚

The estimated sum is ⬚ .

Is your answer reasonable?

Find the difference. Then use front-end estimation to check that your answer is reasonable.

14 Find $715 - 586$.

$715 - 586 = \boxed{}$

$715 - 586$

$\downarrow \qquad \downarrow$

$\boxed{} - \boxed{} = \boxed{}$

The estimated difference is $\boxed{}$.

Is your answer reasonable?

Solve. Check that your answer is reasonable.

15 Jolene walks 472 m.

Ronald walks 394 m.

Find the total distance they walk.

$472 + 394 = \boxed{}$

$472 + 394$

$\downarrow \qquad \downarrow$

$\boxed{} + \boxed{} = \boxed{}$

The estimated distance is $\boxed{}$.

Is your answer reasonable?

16 Mr. Morris sells 726 oranges on a day.

Mrs. Morris sells 654 oranges on the same day.

How many more oranges does Mr. Morris sell?

$726 - 654 = \boxed{}$

$726 - 654$

$\downarrow \qquad \downarrow$

$\boxed{} - \boxed{} = \boxed{}$

The estimated difference is $\boxed{}$.

Is your answer reasonable?

Let's Practice

Name the leading digit in each number.

1 487 ____   **2** 354 ____   **3** 5,762 ____

4 6,735 ____   **5** 8,649 ____   **6** 9,582 ____

Find each sum. Then use front-end estimation to check that your answer is reasonable.

7 354 + 187 = ____   **8** 742 + 254 = ____   **9** 665 + 168 = ____

Find each difference. Then use front-end estimation to check that your answer is reasonable.

10 673 − 154 = ____   **11** 574 − 487 = ____   **12** 739 − 572 = ____

Solve. Use front and estimation to estimate.

13 Jennifer has $228. She needs $654 more to buy a television set. Estimate the cost of the television set.

14 In January, Mr. Estrada's water bill is $47.
In February, his water bill increased to $89.
Estimate how much more his water bill for February is.

ON YOUR OWN

Go to Workbook A:
Practice 4, page 31–34

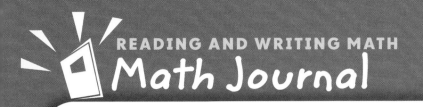

Look at the estimates.
Decide if you agree. Explain your answer.

1 683 + 568 is about 600 + 600.

So, 683 + 568 is about 1,200.

Explanation:

2 510 − 257 is about 500 − 200.

So, 510 − 257 is about 300.

Explanation:

CRITICAL THINKING SKILLS
Put On Your Thinking Cap!

PROBLEM SOLVING

Jean has two 3-digit numbers.

She uses front-end estimation to estimate the sum of the two numbers. Her estimated answer is 800.

Find 3 possible sets of two numbers that are not more than 500 each.

Show your work.

ON YOUR OWN

Go to Workbook A:
Put on Your Thinking Cap!
pages 37–38

Chapter Wrap Up

Study Guide
You have learned...

Mental Math and Estimation

Mental Addition	Mental Subtraction	More Mental Addition

Mental Addition

Add the tens, then add the ones.
Find 36 + 41.

36 + 40 = 76

76 + 1 = 77

So, 36 + 41 = 77.

Add the tens, then subtract the extra ones.
Find 36 + 46.

36 + 50 = 86

86 − 4 = 82

So, 36 + 46 = 82.

Mental Subtraction

Subtract the tens, then subtract the ones.
Find 55 − 23.

55 − 20 = 35

35 − 3 = 32

So, 55 − 23 = 32.

Subtract the tens, then add the extra ones.
Find 72 − 37.

72 − 40 = 32

32 + 3 = 35

So, 72 − 37 = 35.

More Mental Addition

Add 100, then subtract the extra ones.
Find 39 + 96.

39 + 100 = 139

139 − 4 = 135

So, 39 + 96 = 135.

Add the hundreds, then subtract the extra ones.
Find 97 + 98.

100 + 100 = 200

200 − 3 − 2 = 195

So, 97 + 98 = 195.

BIG IDEA

▶ Number bonds and estimation strategies can be used to find and check sums and differences.

Estimation

To estimate
- the sum of two numbers using rounding or front-end estimation
- the difference between two numbers using rounding or front-end estimation.

To use the estimated sums or differences to check that exact answers are reasonable.

Rounded to nearest hundred	**Front-end estimation**
Round to the nearest hundred, then add or subtract. Find $365 + 519$.	Use the value of the leading digits to add or subtract. Find $365 + 519$
$365 + 519 = 884$	$365 + 519 = 884$
365 rounds to 400. 519 rounds to 500. $400 + 500 = 900$	$\begin{array}{ccc} 365 & + & 519 \\ \downarrow & & \downarrow \\ 300 & + & 500 = 800 \end{array}$
884 is about 900. So, the answer is reasonable.	884 is about 800. So, the answer is reasonable.
Find $769 - 314$.	Find $769 - 314$
$769 - 314 = 455$	$769 - 314 = 455$
769 rounds to 800. 314 rounds to 300. $800 - 300 = 500$	$\begin{array}{ccc} 769 & - & 314 \\ \downarrow & & \downarrow \\ 700 & - & 300 = 400 \end{array}$
455 is about 500. So, the answer is reasonable.	455 is about 400. So, the answer is reasonable.

Chapter Review/Test

Vocabulary

Choose the correct word.

rounded
estimated
front-end estimation
leading digit

1 677 is about 700 when [____] to the nearest hundred.

2 The [____] in a number is the digit with the greatest place value.

3 [____] uses the leading digit to estimate a sum or a difference.

Concepts and Skills

Add mentally.

4 27 + 62 = [____]

5 47 + 86 = [____].

6 39 + 96 = [____].

7 98 + 95 = [____].

Subtract mentally.

8 87 − 62 = [____]

9 65 − 27 = [____].

10 53 − 11 = [____]

11 98 − 44 = [____]

Find each sum or difference. Then use rounding to check that your answer is reasonable.

12 215 + 143 =

13 564 + 994 =

14 615 − 323 =

15 864 − 702 =

Find each sum or difference. Then use front-end estimation to check that your answer is reasonable.

16 632 + 421 =

17 636 − 519 =

Problem Solving

Solve. Find the estimate.

18 Paul has 72 cards. He gives away 59 cards. About how many cards does he have left?

19 Rick has $99. He saves another $46. Estimate the amount of money he has now.

20 The Drama Club has $416 to spend on the next play. Costumes cost $185. Make up costs $176. Estimate the total cost of costumes and make-up. Estimate the amount of money left after buying the two items.

3 Addition up to 10,000

Knock! Knock!
Who's there?
One more.
One more who?
One more to add to 99.
And now we have 100!

Knock! Knock!
Who's there?
One more.
One more who?
One more to add to 999.
And now we have 1,000!

Knock! Knock!
Who's there?
One more.
One more who?
One more to add to 9,999.
And now we have 10,000!

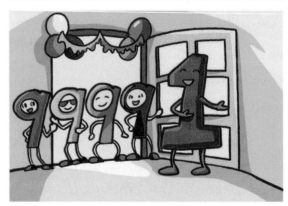

Lessons

3.1 Addition Without Regrouping

3.2 Addition with Regrouping in Hundreds

3.3 Addition with Regrouping in Ones, Tens, and Hundreds

BIG IDEA

▶ Greater numbers can be added the same way 2-digit numbers are added, with or without regrouping.

Recall Prior Knowledge

Finding the sum

45 + 23 = ?

```
    4 5
  + 2 3
    6 8  ← sum
```

The sum of 45 and 23 is 68.

Adding 3-digit numbers without regrouping

452 + 235 = ?

Step 1 Add the ones.

```
    4 5 2
  + 2 3 5
        7
```

Step 2 Add the tens.

```
    4 5 2
  + 2 3 5
      8 7
```

Step 3 Add the hundreds.

```
    4 5 2
  + 2 3 5
    6 8 7
```

Adding 3-digit numbers with regrouping

243 + 178 = ?

Step 1   Add the ones.
Regroup the ones.

```
      1
    2 4 3
  + 1 7 8
        1
```

3 ones + 8 ones
= 11 ones
= 1 ten 1 one

Step 2   Add the tens.
Regroup the tens.

```
    1 1
    2 4 3
  + 1 7 8
      2 1
```

1 ten + 4 tens + 7 tens
= 12 tens
= 1 hundred 2 tens

Step 3   Add the hundreds.

```
    1 1
    2 4 3
  + 1 7 8
    4 2 1
```

1 hundred + 2 hundreds +
1 hundred
= 4 hundreds

Find the sum.

1 The sum of 5 and 4 is ⬚ .

2 The sum of 3 and 15 is ⬚ .

3 The sum of 78 and 21 is ⬚ .

4 The sum of 96 and 123 is ⬚ .

Add.

5 813 + 172 = ⬚

6 654 + 312 = ⬚

7 508 + 271 = ⬚

Add.

8 635 + 249 = ⬚

9 188 + 396 = ⬚

10 217 + 397 = ⬚

3.1 Addition Without Regrouping

Lesson Objective

- Add greater numbers without regrouping.

Learn **Use base-ten blocks and a place-value chart to find the sum.**

Find the **sum** of 1,482 and 7,516.

Thousands	Hundreds	Tens	Ones

The sum of 1,482 and 7,516 is 8,998.

When you add numbers, the answer is the sum of the numbers.

Step 1
Add the ones.

$$\begin{array}{r} 1,48\boxed{2} \\ +\ 7,51\boxed{6} \\ \hline \boxed{8} \end{array}$$

Step 2
Add the tens.

$$\begin{array}{r} 1,4\boxed{8}2 \\ +\ 7,5\boxed{1}6 \\ \hline \boxed{9}8 \end{array}$$

Step 3
Add the hundreds.

$$\begin{array}{r} 1,\boxed{4}82 \\ +\ 7,\boxed{5}16 \\ \hline \boxed{9}98 \end{array}$$

Step 4
Add the thousands.

$$\begin{array}{r} \boxed{1},482 \\ +\ \boxed{7},516 \\ \hline \boxed{8},998 \end{array}$$

Guided Practice

Find the missing numbers.

1 The sum of 2,653 and 3,302 is [ ] .

Thousands	Hundreds	Tens	Ones
2	6	5	3
+ 3	3	0	2
[ ]	[ ]	[ ]	[ ]

Add. Use base-ten blocks to help you.

2
```
  1,693
+ 5,204
  [    ]
```

3
```
  4,025
+   364
  [    ]
```

4
```
  7,143
+ 1,602
  [    ]
```

5
```
  2,700
+ 3,295
  [    ]
```

Let's Practice

Add. Use base-ten blocks to help you.

1 The sum of 436 and 9,210 is [ ] .

2 The sum of 2,421 and 6,308 is [ ] .

3 The sum of 5,668 and 3,020 is [ ] .

ON YOUR OWN

Go to Workbook A:
Practice 1, pages 45–48

Addition with Regrouping in Hundreds

Lesson Objective

- Add greater numbers with regrouping in hundreds.

Vocabulary
regroup

Learn **Use base-ten blocks and a place-value chart to regroup when you add.**

$1,200 + 2,900 = ?$

Thousands	Hundreds	Tens	Ones

Step 1
Add the hundreds.

$$\begin{array}{r} \overset{1}{1},200 \\ +\ 2,900 \\ \hline 100 \end{array}$$

2 hundreds
+ 9 hundreds
= 11 hundreds

Regroup the hundreds.

11 hundreds
= 1 thousand
1 hundred

Thousands	Hundreds	Tens	Ones

Step 2
Add the thousands.

$$\begin{array}{r} \overset{1}{1},200 \\ +\ 2,900 \\ \hline 4,100 \end{array}$$

1 thousand
+ 1 thousand
+ 2 thousands
= 4 thousands

The sum of 1,200 and 2,900 is 4,100.

Guided Practice

Find the missing numbers. Use base-ten blocks to help you.

1 4,500 + 3,800 = ?

First, add the hundreds and regroup.

5 hundreds + 8 hundreds = [ ] hundreds

= [ ] thousand [ ] hundreds

$$\begin{array}{r} 4,500 \\ + 3,800 \\ \hline \end{array}$$

Then, add the thousands.

[ ] thousand + 4 thousands + 3 thousands = [ ] thousands

So, 4,500 + 3,800 = [ ] .

Add. Use base-ten blocks to help you.

2
$$\begin{array}{r} 5,300 \\ + 1,900 \\ \hline \end{array}$$

3
$$\begin{array}{r} 2,800 \\ + 1,700 \\ \hline \end{array}$$

4
$$\begin{array}{r} 7,923 \\ + 1,541 \\ \hline \end{array}$$

5
$$\begin{array}{r} 3,840 \\ + 4,720 \\ \hline \end{array}$$

Find the sum of these numbers.

6 4,800 and 4,700 [ ]

7 4,300 and 2,800 [ ]

8 3,500 and 6,500 [ ]

9 2,473 and 1,623 [ ]

Players: **4 to 6**
Materials:
- hundreds cards from 100 to 900 (four sets)

Snap-a-Thousand!

STEP 1 Cut out hundreds cards from 100 to 900.
You have four cards for each number.

STEP 2 Mix up the cards.
Each player draws six cards.

STEP 3 Each player shows one card at the same time.

STEP 4 Softly say "Snap-a-Thousand" when you see two cards which add to 1,000.

Example
1,000

STEP 5 The first player to say "Snap-a-Thousand" collects the two cards.

When no more thousand pairs can be found, all players show their next card and continue the game.

STEP 6 End the game when no more cards add to 1,000.

The player who collects the most pairs wins!

Let's Explore!

WORK IN PAIRS

For each sum, find a digit that will result in regrouping in the hundreds place. Then add.

Example

```
    1
  4, 2 0 0
+ 2, ? 0 0
```

> If I put 1, 2, 3, 4, 5, 6, or 7 in the box, I can't regroup the hundreds. Let me try 8 or 9.

Using the digit '8'

```
    1
  4, 2 0 0
+ 2, 8 0 0
      0 0 0
```
Add the hundreds first.

```
    1
  4, 2 0 0
+ 2, 8 0 0
  7, 0 0 0
```
Then, add the thousands.
The sum is 7,000.

Using the digit '9'

```
    1
  4, 2 0 0
+ 2, 9 0 0
      1 0 0
```
Add the hundreds first.

> The number can be 8 or 9!

```
    1
  4, 2 0 0
+ 2, 9 0 0
  7, 1 0 0
```
Then, add the thousands.
The sum is 7,100.

1
```
  5,    0 0
+ 2, 6 0 0
```

2
```
  2, 4 0 0
+ 3,    0 0
```

3
```
  6, 8 0 0
+ 2,    0 0
```

Let's Practice

Find the sum of these numbers.

1 The sum of 4,400 and 2,700 is _____ .

2 The sum of 3,500 and 5,500 is _____ .

3 The sum of 2,600 and 1,600 is _____ .

**Add. Use base-ten blocks to help you.
Find the missing numbers.**

4
$$\begin{array}{r} 2,473 \\ +\ 1,623 \\ \hline \end{array}$$

5
$$\begin{array}{r} 4,561 \\ +\ 2,728 \\ \hline \end{array}$$

6
$$\begin{array}{r} 4,422 \\ +\ 2,614 \\ \hline \end{array}$$

7
$$\begin{array}{r} 5,674 \\ +\ 3,811 \\ \hline \end{array}$$

8
$$\begin{array}{r} 2,822 \\ +\ 2,753 \\ \hline \end{array}$$

9
$$\begin{array}{r} 1,462 \\ +\ 3,732 \\ \hline \end{array}$$

ON YOUR OWN

**Go to Workbook A:
Practice 2, pages 49–50**

Lesson 3.3 Addition with Regrouping in Ones, Tens, and Hundreds

Lesson Objective

- Add greater numbers with regrouping in ones, tens, and hundreds.

Learn **Sometimes you regroup more than once.**

$1,153 + 4,959 = ?$

Thousands	Hundreds	Tens	Ones

Step 1
Add the ones.

$$
\begin{array}{r}
1,1\overset{1}{5}\,3 \\
+\ 4,9\,5\,9 \\
\hline
2 \\
\end{array}
$$

3 ones + 9 ones
= 12 ones

Regroup the ones.
12 ones
= 1 ten 2 ones

Thousands	Hundreds	Tens	Ones

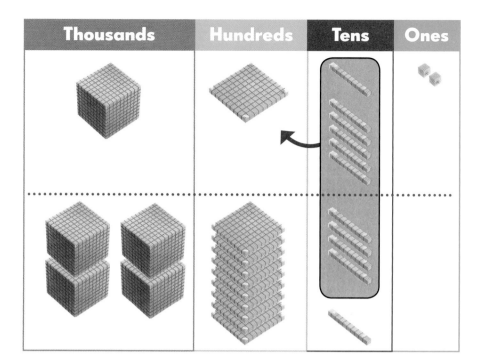

Step 2
Add the tens.

$$
\begin{array}{r}
\overset{1}{1,}\; \overset{1}{1}\; \overset{1}{5}\; 3 \\
+\; 4,\; 9\; 5\; 9 \\
\hline
1\; 2
\end{array}
$$

1 ten + 5 tens
+ 5 tens
= 11 tens

Regroup the tens.
11 tens
= 1 hundred 1 ten

Thousands	Hundreds	Tens	Ones

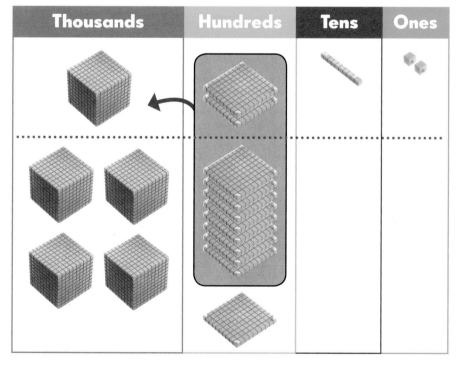

Step 3
Add the hundreds.

$$
\begin{array}{r}
\overset{1}{1,}\; \overset{1}{1}\; \overset{1}{5}\; 3 \\
+\; 4,\; 9\; 5\; 9 \\
\hline
1\; 1\; 2
\end{array}
$$

1 hundred
+ 1 hundred
+ 9 hundreds
= 11 hundreds

Regroup the hundreds.
11 hundreds
= 1 thousand
1 hundred

Continued on next page

Thousands	Hundreds	Tens	Ones

The sum of 1,153 and 4,959 is 6,112.

Step 4

Add the thousands.

$$
\begin{array}{r}
{\scriptstyle 1}\ {\scriptstyle 1}\ {\scriptstyle 1} \\
1,\ 1\ 5\ 3 \\
+\ 4,\ 9\ 5\ 9 \\
\hline
6,\ 1\ 1\ 2
\end{array}
$$

1 thousand
+ 1 thousand
+ 4 thousands
= 6 thousands

Guided Practice

Add. Use base-ten blocks to help you.

1
$$
\begin{array}{r}
3,6\ 2\ 8 \\
+\ 1,7\ 9\ 5 \\
\hline
\end{array}
$$

2
$$
\begin{array}{r}
5,3\ 4\ 8 \\
+\ 3,7\ 9\ 2 \\
\hline
\end{array}
$$

Solve.

3 One year, the population of Crystal Town is 7,325. Within the same year, 2,501 people move into the town. How many people are now in Crystal Town?

4 Mr. Streep makes 4,728 dinner rolls in a day. Mr. Wu makes 1,584 more dinner rolls than Mr. Streep. How many dinner rolls does Mr. Wu make?

help you.

is ☐ .

is ☐ .

4 1,628 + 4,586 = ☐

Solve.

5 Cathy and Jordan take a walk through the forest.
Cathy takes Route A and Jordan takes Route B.
There are 3 places where Route A and Route B cross.
They agree to meet at each place to add the two numbers
that they see along the way.
Find the three answers.

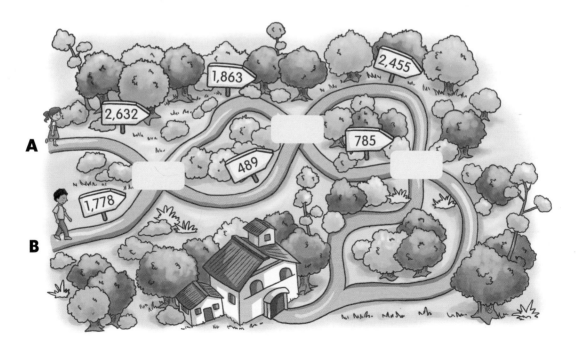

ON YOUR OWN

Go to Workbook A:
Practice 3, pages 51–54

Math Journal

Look at the addition problems. Explain the error in each.

Example

```
   3, 4 6 7
+  1, 9 3 2
   4, 3 9 9
```

Error: The hundreds were not regrouped into thousands and hundreds.

```
   7, 5 2 9
+  2, 4 6 1
   9, 9 8 0
```

Error: The ones were not regrouped into tens and ones.

1
```
   5, 8 6 9
+  1, 4 2 5
   4, 4 4 4
```

2
```
   3, 5 7 3
+  1, 6 4 5
   4, 1 1 8
```

List the steps for adding these two numbers.

Example

```
    1
   2 3 4
+  4 7 5
   7 0 9
```

Step 1
Add 4 ones and 5 ones to get 9 ones.

Step 2
Add 3 tens and 7 tens to get 10 tens.

Step 3
Regroup 10 tens into 1 hundred and 0 tens.

Step 4
Add 1 hundred, 2 hundreds, and 4 hundreds to get 7 hundreds.

3
```
   4, 2 6 7
+  2, 9 1 5
```

Put On Your Thinking Cap!

PROBLEM SOLVING

Find the sum of the numbers.
Use number bonds to help you find a number pattern.

Example

$320 + 182 + 260 + 242 + 160 + 342 + 360 +$
$142 + 190 + 312 = ?$

$320 + 182 = 500 + 2$
$260 + 242 = 500 + 2$
$160 + 342 = 500 + 2$
$360 + 142 = 500 + 2$
$190 + 312 = 500 + 2$

Look for a pattern.

Five 500s + five 2s
$= 2,500 + 10$
$= 2,510$

1. $360 + 645 + 720 + 285 + 430 + 575 +$
$810 + 195 = ?$

ON YOUR OWN

Go to Workbook A:
Put on Your Thinking Cap!
pages 55–58

Chapter Wrap Up

Study Guide
You have learned...

BIG IDEA

► Greater numbers can be added the same way 2-digit numbers are added, with or without regrouping.

Addition up to 10,000

Without Regrouping	With Regrouping

Without Regrouping

$2,315 + 1,231 = 3,546$

$$
\begin{array}{r}
2,3\ 1\ 5 \\
+\ 1,2\ 3\ 1 \\
\hline
3,5\ 4\ 6
\end{array}
$$

Step 1 Add the ones.
5 ones + 1 one
= 6 ones

Step 2 Add the tens.
1 ten + 3 tens
= 4 tens

Step 3 Add the hundreds.
3 hundreds
+ 2 hundreds
= 5 hundreds

Step 4 Add the thousands.
2 thousands
+ 1 thousand
= 3 thousands

With Regrouping

$1,434 + 4,567 = 6,001$

$$
\begin{array}{r}
{\scriptstyle 1\ \ 1\ \ 1} \\
1,4\ 3\ 4 \\
+\ 4,5\ 6\ 7 \\
\hline
6,0\ 0\ 1
\end{array}
$$

Step 1 Add the ones and regroup.
4 ones + 7 ones
= 11 ones
= 1 ten 1 one

Step 2 Add the tens and regroup.
1 ten + 3 tens + 6 tens
= 10 tens
= 1 hundred 0 tens

Step 3 Add the hundreds and regroup.
1 hundred + 4 hundreds
+ 5 hundreds
= 10 hundreds
= 1 thousand 0 hundreds

Step 4 Add the thousands.
1 thousand + 1 thousand
+ 4 thousands
= 6 thousands

Chapter Review/Test

Vocabulary

Choose the correct word.

sum

addition

regroup

1 When you _____ 23 ones, you get 2 tens 3 ones.

2 When you add two or more numbers, the answer is the _____ .

Concepts and Skills

Add.

3
$$
\begin{array}{r}
3,112 \\
+\quad 635 \\
\hline
\end{array}
$$

4
$$
\begin{array}{r}
5,618 \\
+\ 2,045 \\
\hline
\end{array}
$$

5
$$
\begin{array}{r}
2,573 \\
+\ 1,989 \\
\hline
\end{array}
$$

6
$$
\begin{array}{r}
6,725 \\
+\ 2,805 \\
\hline
\end{array}
$$

Find the sum.

7 The sum of 6,213 and 2,418 is _____ .

8 The sum of 4,283 and 2,974 is _____ .

Problem Solving

Solve.

9 Baker Elliot bakes 2,925 buns in three months.
He bakes 1,861 fewer buns than Baker Susan.
How many buns does Baker Susan bake?

10 3,695 children visit the art museum in January.
816 more children visit the art museum in February than in January.
How many children visit the museum in February?

Subtraction up to 10,000

Lessons

BIG IDEA

▶ Greater numbers can be subtracted with or without regrouping.

Finding the difference

70 − 12 = ?

$$\begin{array}{r} \overset{6}{\cancel{7}}{}^{1}0 \\ -\ 1\ 2 \\ \hline 5\ 8 \end{array}$$ ←— difference

The difference between 70 and 12 is 58.

Subtracting 3-digit numbers without regrouping

859 − 325 = ?

Step 1 Subtract the ones.

$$\begin{array}{r} 8\ 5\ 9 \\ -\ 3\ 2\ 5 \\ \hline 4 \end{array}$$

Step 2 Subtract the tens.

$$\begin{array}{r} 8\ 5\ 9 \\ -\ 3\ 2\ 5 \\ \hline 3\ 4 \end{array}$$

Step 3 Subtract the hundreds.

$$\begin{array}{r} 8\ 5\ 9 \\ -\ 3\ 2\ 5 \\ \hline 5\ 3\ 4 \end{array}$$

Subtracting 3-digit numbers with regrouping

$$\begin{array}{r} \overset{4}{\cancel{5}}\ \overset{1}{\cancel{2}}{}^{1}3 \\ -\ 1\ 4\ 8 \\ \hline 3\ 7\ 5 \end{array}$$

Step 1 Regroup the tens and ones. Subtract the ones.

Step 2 Regroup the hundreds and tens. Subtract the tens.

Step 3 Subtract the hundreds.

✔**Quick Check**

Find the difference.
Subtract.

1 The difference between 162 and 29 is ⬚ .

2 368 − 153 = ⬚

3 714 − 359 = ⬚

4.1 Subtraction Without Regrouping

Lesson Objective

• Use base-ten blocks to subtract without regrouping.

Vocabulary
difference

Learn **Use base-ten blocks and a place-value chart to find the difference .**

Find the difference between 4,368 and 1,254.

Thousands	Hundreds	Tens	Ones

Thousands	Hundreds	Tens	Ones

The difference between 4,368 and 1,254 is 3,114.

Step 1
Subtract the ones.

$$\begin{array}{r} 4,36\,8 \\ -\ 1,25\,4 \\ \hline 4 \end{array}$$

Step 2
Subtract the tens.

$$\begin{array}{r} 4,3\,68 \\ -\ 1,2\,54 \\ \hline 1\,4 \end{array}$$

Step 3
Subtract the hundreds.

$$\begin{array}{r} 4,368 \\ -\ 1,254 \\ \hline 1\,1\,4 \end{array}$$

Step 4
Subtract the thousands.

$$\begin{array}{r} 4,368 \\ -\ 1,254 \\ \hline 3,1\,1\,4 \end{array}$$

When you subtract numbers, the answer is the difference.

Check!

If 4,368 − 1,254 = 3,114,
then 3,114 + 1,254 should equal
4,368.
The answer is correct.

$$\begin{array}{r} 3,114 \\ +\ 1,254 \\ \hline 4,368 \end{array}$$

Guided Practice

Find the missing numbers.

1. The difference between 7,526 and 2,103 is _____ .

Thousands	Hundreds	Tens	Ones
7	5	2	6
− 2	1	0	3

Subtract. Use base-ten blocks to help you.

2.
$$\begin{array}{r} 2,356 \\ -\ 1,243 \\ \hline \end{array}$$

Add to check your answers.

3.
$$\begin{array}{r} 3,418 \\ -\ 3,102 \\ \hline \end{array}$$

4.
$$\begin{array}{r} 9,832 \\ -\ 7,810 \\ \hline \end{array}$$

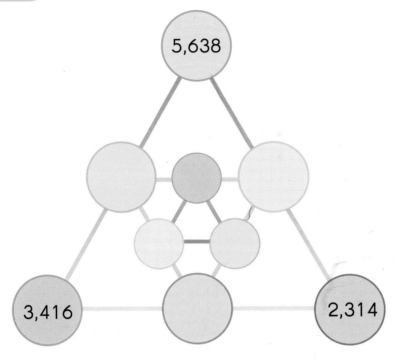

^{STEP}
1 Use the figure provided. Choose two numbers from the figure. Subtract the number that is less from the greater number. Use base-ten blocks to help you.

^{STEP}
2 Write the answer in the circle between the two numbers.

^{STEP}
3 Repeat **1** and **2** until you fill in all the circles.

Let's Practice

Subtract.

1. 3,678
    − 2,417

2. 4,853
    − 1,121

3. 5,942
    − 3,732

4. 9,603
    − 5,501

5. The difference between 4,298 and 2,045 is [____].

6. The difference between 5,138 and 7,459 is [____].

7. 4,786 − 2,534 = [____]

8. 9,205 − 6,102 = [____]

Add to check your answers.

ON YOUR OWN

Go to Workbook A:
Practice 1, pages 59–60

Subtraction with Regrouping in Hundreds and Thousands

Lesson Objective

• Use base-ten blocks to subtract with regrouping.

Vocabulary
regroup

Learn **Use base-ten blocks and a place-value chart to subtract with regrouping.**

3,249 − 1,926 = ?

Thousands	Hundreds	Tens	Ones

Step 1
Subtract the ones.

$$\begin{array}{r} 3,24\boxed{9} \\ -\ 1,92\boxed{6} \\ \hline \boxed{3} \end{array}$$

9 ones − 6 ones = 3 ones

Thousands	Hundreds	Tens	Ones

Step 2
Subtract the tens.

$$\begin{array}{r} 3,2\boxed{4}9 \\ -\ 1,9\boxed{2}6 \\ \hline \boxed{2}3 \end{array}$$

4 tens − 2 tens = 2 tens

Thousands	Hundreds	Tens	Ones

$$\begin{array}{r} 3,2\,4\,9 \\ -\ 1,9\,2\,6 \\ \hline 2\,3 \end{array}$$

9 hundreds cannot be subtracted from 2 hundreds. So, **regroup** the thousands and hundreds.

Thousands	Hundreds	Tens	Ones

Regroup.
3 thousands 2 hundreds
= 2 thousands 12 hundreds

Continued on next page

Thousands	Hundreds	Tens	Ones

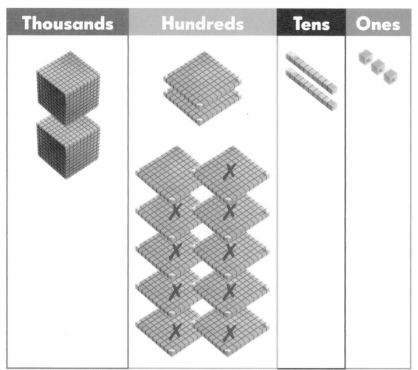

Step 3
Subtract the hundreds.

$$\begin{array}{r} \overset{2}{\cancel{3}},\overset{1}{}2\,4\,9 \\ -\ 1,9\,2\,6 \\ \hline 3\,2\,3 \end{array}$$

12 hundreds − 9 hundreds
= 3 hundreds

Thousands	Hundreds	Tens	Ones

Step 4
Subtract
the thousands.

$$\begin{array}{r} \overset{2}{\cancel{3}},\overset{1}{}2\,4\,9 \\ -\ 1,9\,2\,6 \\ \hline 1,3\,2\,3 \end{array}$$

2 thousands − 1 thousand
= 1 thousand

When 1,926 is subtracted from 3,249, the difference is 1,323.

Check!

If 3,249 − 1,926 = 1,323,
then 1,323 + 1,926 should equal 3,249.
The answer is correct.

$$\begin{array}{r} \overset{1}{}1,3\,2\,3 \\ +\ 1,9\,2\,6 \\ \hline 3,2\,4\,9 \end{array}$$

Guided Practice

Regroup. Find the missing numbers.

1. 7 thousands 3 hundreds = 6 thousands [ ] hundreds

2. 4 thousands 1 hundred − 2 thousands 8 hundreds

   = 3 thousands [ ] hundreds − 2 thousands 8 hundreds

   = 1 thousand [ ] hundreds

Subtract. Use base-ten blocks to help you.

3.
```
   6, 2 0 0
 −    8 0 0
```

4.
```
   5, 1 2 6
 − 3, 4 1 2
```

5.
```
   8, 4 1 5
 − 6, 7 0 5
```

Let's Practice

Add to check your answers.

Find the difference. Use base-ten blocks to help you.

1. The difference between 4,600 and 2,800 is [ ].

2. The difference between 5,678 and 742 is [ ].

3. The difference between 5,523 and 7,243 is [ ].

Subtract.

4.
```
   5, 2 2 1
 − 3, 4 1 0
```

5.
```
   8, 7 3 5
 − 2, 8 1 2
```

ON YOUR OWN

**Go to Workbook A:
Practice 2, pages 61–62**

Lesson 4.3 Subtraction with Regrouping in Ones, Tens, Hundreds, and Thousands

Lesson Objective

- Use base-ten blocks to subtract with regrouping.

Learn **Use base-ten blocks and a place-value chart to subtract with regrouping.**

$5,146 - 2,598 = ?$

$$\begin{array}{r} 5,146 \\ -\ 2,598 \end{array}$$

8 ones cannot be subtracted from 6 ones. So, regroup the tens and ones.

Regroup.
4 tens 6 ones
= 3 tens 16 ones

Thousands	Hundreds	Tens	Ones

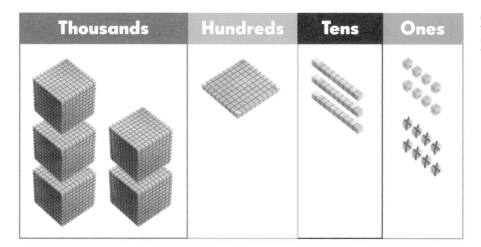

Step 1
Subtract the ones.

$$\begin{array}{r} 5,1\ \overset{3}{\cancel{4}}\ \overset{1}{6} \\ -\ 2,5\ 9\ 8 \\ \hline 8 \end{array}$$

16 ones − 8 ones
= 8 ones

$$\begin{array}{r} 5,1\ \overset{3}{\cancel{4}}\ \overset{1}{6} \\ -\ 2,5\ 9\ 8 \\ \hline 8 \end{array}$$

9 tens cannot
be subtracted
from 3 tens.
So, regroup
the hundreds
and tens.

Regroup.
1 hundred 3 tens
= 0 hundreds 13 tens

Continued on next page

Lesson 4.3 Subtraction with Regrouping in Ones, Tens, Hundreds, and Thousands **103**

Thousands	Hundreds	Tens	Ones
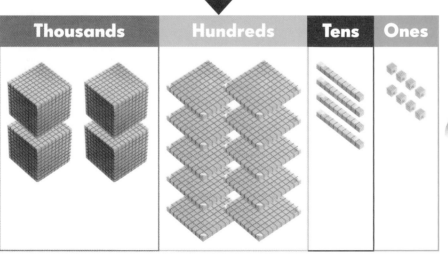			

Step 2

Subtract the tens.

$$5, \overset{0}{\cancel{1}} \, \overset{1\,3}{\cancel{4}} \, 6$$
$$-\ 2,5\ 9\ 8$$
$$\underline{4\ 8}$$

13 tens − 9 tens
= 4 tens

Thousands	Hundreds	Tens	Ones

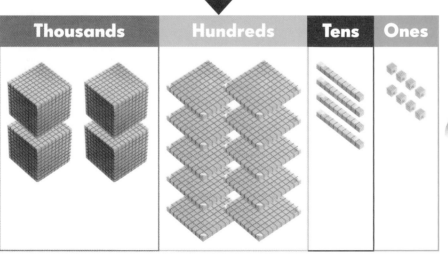

$$5, \overset{0}{\cancel{1}} \, \overset{1\,3}{\cancel{4}} \, 6$$
$$-\ 2,5\ 9\ 8$$
$$\underline{4\ 8}$$

5 hundreds cannot be subtracted from 0 hundreds. So, regroup the thousands and hundreds.

Regroup.
5 thousands 0 hundreds
= 4 thousands
    10 hundreds

Thousands	Hundreds	Tens	Ones

Step 3

Subtract the
hundreds.

$$
\begin{array}{r}
{}^4\,{}^{1}0\,{}^{1}3 \\
5,\cancel{1}4\,\cancel{1}6 \\
-\ 2,5\,9\,8 \\
\hline
5\,4\,8
\end{array}
$$

10 hundreds
− 5 hundreds
= 5 hundreds

Thousands	Hundreds	Tens	Ones

Step 4

Subtract the
thousands.

$$
\begin{array}{r}
{}^4\,{}^{1}0\,{}^{1}3 \\
\cancel{5},\cancel{1}4\,\cancel{1}6 \\
-\ 2,5\,9\,8 \\
\hline
2,5\,4\,8
\end{array}
$$

4 thousands
− 2 thousands
= 2 thousands

The difference between 5,146 and 2,598 is 2,548.

Check!

If 5,146 − 2,598 = 2,548,
then 2,548 + 2,598 should equal 5,146.
The answer is correct.

$$
\begin{array}{r}
{}^1\ \ {}^1\ \ {}^1 \\
2,5\,4\,8 \\
+\ 2,5\,9\,8 \\
\hline
5,1\,4\,6
\end{array}
$$

Guided Practice

Regroup. Find the missing numbers.

1 5 hundreds 8 tens = 4 hundreds [   ] tens

2 9 hundreds 3 tens 2 ones − 4 hundreds 4 tens 4 ones
= 9 hundreds [   ] tens [   ] ones − 4 hundreds 4 tens 4 ones
= 8 hundreds [   ] tens 12 ones − 4 hundreds 4 tens 4 ones

Subtract. Use base-ten blocks to help you.

3
$$\begin{array}{r} 5,176 \\ -\ 4,378 \\ \hline \end{array}$$

4
$$\begin{array}{r} 6,452 \\ -\ 2,783 \\ \hline \end{array}$$

5
$$\begin{array}{r} 8,324 \\ -\ 5,786 \\ \hline \end{array}$$

Let's Practice

Find the difference. Use base-ten blocks to help you.

1 The difference between 8,240 and 3,971 is [   ].

2 The difference between 6,130 and 2,580 is [   ].

3 The difference between 9,162 and 467 is [   ].

4 The difference between 3,210 and 1,789 is [   ].

5 The difference between 2,310 and 1,627 is [   ].

6 The difference between 4,692 and 893 is [   ].

Add to check your answers.

ON YOUR OWN

Go to Workbook A:
Practice 3, pages 63–66

Go for the Smallest!

Players: **2 to 4**
Materials:
- seven sets of number cards from 0 to 9

STEP **1** Cut out seven sets of number cards from 0 to 9.

STEP **2** Mix up the cards. Each player turns eight cards face up.

STEP **3** Arrange your cards so that you get two 4-digit numbers.

STEP **4** Subtract the numbers. The player with the least difference scores 5 points. Play three rounds.

The player with the most points wins!

Subtraction Across Zeros

Lesson Objectives

- Use base-ten blocks to subtract across zeros.
- Write subtraction number sentences.
- Solve subtraction word problems.

Learn **Use base-ten blocks when subtracting across zeros.**

2,000 − 257 = ?

Regroup the thousands and hundreds.

Regroup.
2 thousands
= 1 thousand 10 hundreds

Regroup the hundreds and tens.

Regroup.
10 hundreds
= 9 hundreds 10 tens

Thousands	Hundreds	Tens	Ones

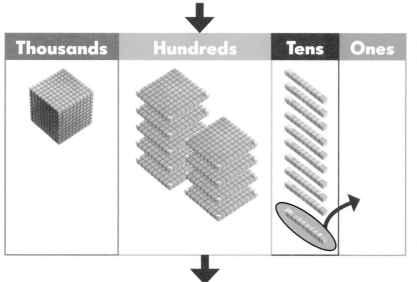

Regroup the tens and ones.

Regroup.
10 tens = 9 tens 10 ones

Thousands	Hundreds	Tens	Ones

Thousands	Hundreds	Tens	Ones

Step 1
Subtract the ones.

$$
\begin{array}{r}
\overset{1}{\cancel{2}}\ \overset{19}{\cancel{0}}\ \overset{19}{\cancel{0}}\ \overset{1}{0} \\
-\ \ 2\ 5\ 7 \\
\hline
3
\end{array}
$$

10 ones − 7 ones
= 3 ones

Continued on next page

Thousands	Hundreds	Tens	Ones

Step 2

Subtract the tens.

$$\begin{array}{r} 2\,\overset{1}{\cancel{0}}\,\overset{19}{\cancel{0}}\,\overset{19}{\cancel{0}}\,0 \\ -\quad 2\;5\;7 \\ \hline 4\;3 \end{array}$$

9 tens − 5 tens = 4 tens

Thousands	Hundreds	Tens	Ones

Step 3

Subtract the hundreds.

$$\begin{array}{r} 2\,\overset{1}{\cancel{0}}\,\overset{19}{\cancel{0}}\,\overset{19}{\cancel{0}}\,0 \\ -\quad 2\;5\;7 \\ \hline 7\;4\;3 \end{array}$$

9 hundreds − 2 hundreds = 7 hundreds

Thousands	Hundreds	Tens	Ones

Step 4

Subtract the thousands.

$$\begin{array}{r} 2\,\overset{1}{\cancel{0}}\,\overset{19}{\cancel{0}}\,\overset{19}{\cancel{0}}\,0 \\ -\quad 2\;5\;7 \\ \hline 1,7\;4\;3 \end{array}$$

1 thousand − 0 thousands = 1 thousand

The difference between 2,000 and 257 is 1,743.

Can you use estimation to check if your answer is accurate? Explain why or why not.

Guided Practice

Subtract. Use base-ten blocks to help you.

1
$$\begin{array}{r} 5,000 \\ -\ 3,700 \\ \hline \end{array}$$

2
$$\begin{array}{r} 6,000 \\ -\ 4,765 \\ \hline \end{array}$$

Add to check your answers.

3
$$\begin{array}{r} 8,003 \\ -\ 5,147 \\ \hline \end{array}$$

Solve.

4 Simon scores 4,000 points in a game.
Leanne scores 935 fewer points in the game than Simon.
How many points does Leanne score?

5 A store has 2,000 reams of paper and 1,726 notebooks.
How many more reams of paper than notebooks does the store have?

6 3005 types of plants are on display at a flower show.
987 plants are orchids.
How many other types of plants are there?

Players: 4 to 8
Materials:
• Card A and Card B

Subtract the Numbers!

1 Pick one number from Card A and a greater number from Card B.

Card A	Card B
126	1,000
12	2,000
1,645	3,000
3,200	4,000

2 Subtract the number that is less from the greater number.

$$4,000 - 3,200$$

3 Play four rounds.

The group with the most correct answers wins!

Let's Practice

Subtract.

1.
```
    7, 0 0 0
  − 2, 8 4 0
  ─────────
```

2.
```
    3, 0 1 0
  − 2, 7 9 3
  ─────────
```

3.
```
    2, 0 0 5
  − 1, 0 0 7
  ─────────
```

4. The difference between 7,000 and 42 is _____ .

5. The difference between 8,000 and 159 is _____ .

Solve.

6. An art school buys 1,450 ink stamps and 3,000 markers.
   How many more markers than ink stamps does the school buy?

7. Sonya folds 1,000 green and red paper stars.
   692 paper stars are green.
   How many are red?

ON YOUR OWN

Go to Workbook A:
Practice 4, pages 67–68

Math Journal

Explain the errors.
Then find the correct answer.

1
$$\begin{array}{r} 5,406 \\ -\ 3,798 \\ \hline 2,392 \end{array} \text{✗}$$

2
$$\begin{array}{r} 7,285 \\ -\ 3,429 \\ \hline 3,866 \end{array} \text{✗}$$

3
$$\begin{array}{r} 5,128 \\ -\ 4,534 \\ \hline 9,662 \end{array} \text{✗}$$

CRITICAL THINKING SKILLS
Put On Your Thinking Cap!

PROBLEM SOLVING
Find the missing numbers.

1
$$\begin{array}{r} 4,\square\,8\;3 \\ -\ 1,7\;2\,\square \\ \hline \square,8\;5\;7 \end{array}$$

2
$$\begin{array}{r} 7,\square\,5\;1 \\ -\ \square,6\;1\;9 \\ \hline 4,8\;3\,\square \end{array}$$

3
$$\begin{array}{r} \square,0\,\square\,0 \\ -\ 2,6\;4\;3 \\ \hline 2,\square\,5\;7 \end{array}$$

4
$$\begin{array}{r} 8,\square\,4\;0 \\ -\ \square,7\,\square\,9 \\ \hline 4,2\;7\,\square \end{array}$$

ON YOUR OWN

Go to Workbook A:
Put on Your Thinking Cap!
pages 69–72

Chapter Wrap Up

Study Guide
You have learned...

BIG IDEA

▶ Greater numbers can be subtracted with or without regrouping.

Subtraction up to 10,000

Without Regrouping

Subtract the ones.
Subtract the tens.
Subtract the hundreds.
Subtract the thousands.

$$\begin{array}{r} 4,663 \\ -\ 1,231 \\ \hline 3,432 \end{array}$$

Check using addition.
If 4,663 − 1,231 = 3,432,
then 3,432 + 1,231 should equal 4,663.

$$\begin{array}{r} 3,432 \\ +\ 1,231 \\ \hline 4,663 \end{array}$$

With Regrouping

Regroup.
9,876
= 9 thousands 8 hundreds
  7 tens 6 ones
= 9 thousands 8 hundreds 6 tens
  16 ones
= 9 thousands 7 hundreds 16 tens 16 ones
= 8 thousands 17 hundreds 16 tens
  16 ones

$$\begin{array}{r} {}^{8}\,{}^{17}\,{}^{16}\,{}^{1} \\ 9,8\,7\,6 \\ -\ 7,8\,7\,7 \\ \hline 1,9\,9\,9 \end{array}$$

Check using addition.
If 9,876 − 7,877 = 1,999,
then 1,999 + 7,877
should equal 9,876.

$$\begin{array}{r} {}^{1}\ {}^{1}\ {}^{1} \\ 1,9\,9\,9 \\ +\ 7,8\,7\,7 \\ \hline 9,8\,7\,6 \end{array}$$

Regroup.
5,000
= 5 thousands
= 4 thousands 10 hundreds
= 4 thousands 9 hundreds 10 tens
= 4 thousands 9 hundreds 9 tens
  10 ones

$$\begin{array}{r} {}^{4}\ {}^{9}\ {}^{9} \\ 5,\,{}^{1}0\,{}^{1}0\,0 \\ -\ 4,\,3\,2\,1 \\ \hline 6\,7\,9 \end{array}$$

Check using addition.
If 5,000 − 4,321 = 679,
then 679 + 4,321
should equal 5,000.

$$\begin{array}{r} {}^{1}\ {}^{1}\ {}^{1} \\ 6\,7\,9 \\ +\ 4,\,3\,2\,1 \\ \hline 5,\,0\,0\,0 \end{array}$$

Chapter Review/Test

Vocabulary

Choose the correct word.

> subtraction sentence
> regroup
> difference

1 When you subtract numbers, the answer is the _____.

2 You _____ thousands and hundreds when you rewrite 4 thousands as 3 thousands 10 hundreds.

3 A mathematical statement with a minus sign and an equal symbol is an example of a _____.

Concepts and Skills

Subtract.

4
```
   3, 7 4 2
 -    6 3 1
```

5
```
   7, 0 2 5
 - 1, 4 1 3
```

6
```
   4, 3 6 6
 -    7 4 9
```

7
```
   5, 7 8 2
 - 1, 9 1 3
```

8
```
   9, 3 2 6
 - 1, 4 3 8
```

9
```
   1, 0 0 0
 -    7 1 5
```

Problem Solving

Solve.

10 6,000 empty cans are collected in a recycling drive.
3,156 of them are crushed.
How many cans are left?

11 6,206 tickets are available for a concert.
2,078 tickets are sold.
How many tickets are still available?

Using Bar Models: Addition and Subtraction

Lesson

5.1 Real-World Problems: Addition and Subtraction

BIG IDEA

▶ Bar models, addition, and subtraction can be used to solve 2-step real-world problems.

117

Recall Prior Knowledge

Using part-whole bar models to solve real-world problems on addition

Mrs. Jones buys a cake for $15 and has $42 left.
How much money did Mrs. Jones have at first?

$15 + $42 = $57

Mrs. Jones had $57.

Using adding-on bar models to solve real-world problems on addition

Shawn orders 75 boxes of fruit on the first day.
He orders another 84 boxes of fruit on the second day.
How many boxes of fruit does he order on both days?

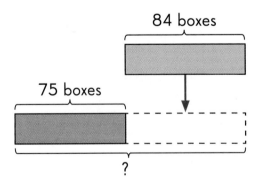

75 + 84 = 159

Shawn orders 159 boxes of fruits on both days.

Using comparison bar models to solve real-world problems on addition

Grant buys 345 fruit bars.
Ken buys 230 more fruit bars than Grant.
How many fruit bars does Ken buy?

$345 + 230 = 575$

Ken buys 575 fruit bars.

Using part-whole bar models to solve real-world problems on subtraction

Ben has 60 baseball cards and football cards in all.
He has 24 football cards.
How many baseball cards does he have?

24 football cards | ? baseball cards

60 baseball and football cards

$60 - 24 = 36$

He has 36 baseball cards.

Using taking-away bar models to solve real-world problems on subtraction

Bob has 110 bottles of water.
He sells 28 bottles of water.
How many bottles of water does he have left?

$$110 - 28 = 82$$

Bob has 82 bottles of water left.

Using comparison bar models to solve real-world problems on subtraction

Tanya reads 749 pages.
Michelle reads 324 fewer pages than Tanya.
How many pages does Michelle read?

$$749 - 324 = 425$$

Michelle reads 425 pages.

Quick Check

Solve. Use bar models to help you.

1. Celeste counts 15 pictures of monkeys and 20 pictures of birds in her book. How many pictures of monkeys and birds does she count?

2. Jonathan reads 121 pages of a book on Saturday. He reads another 59 pages on Sunday. How many pages does he read in the two days?

3. An orchard has 637 apple trees. 360 of the trees grow green apples. How many of the trees grow red apples?

4. A tank holds 546 liters of water. 327 liters of water are poured out. How much water is left in the tank?

5. Sandy has $586. Sandy has $124 less than Peter. How much money does Peter have?

6. A supermarket displays 350 strawberries for sale. On display are 186 more strawberries than oranges. How many oranges are on display?

Lesson 5.1 Real-World Problems: Addition and Subtraction

Lesson Objective

- Use bar models to solve 2-step real-world problems on addition and subtraction.

Vocabulary
sum
difference
bar model

Learn Use bar models and addition or subtraction to solve 2-step real-world problems.

Nancy and Sue sold tickets for a concert.
Nancy sold 3,450 tickets.
Sue sold 1,286 fewer tickets than Nancy.

a How many tickets did Sue sell?

b How many tickets did they sell in all?

3,450 tickets

Nancy

Sue

b ?

a ?   1,286 tickets

Sue sold fewer tickets than Nancy. So, use a comparison model.

a 3,450 − 1,286 = 2,164
Sue sold 2,164 concert tickets.

b 3,450 + 2,164 = 5,614
They sold 5,614 concert tickets in all.

Check!

2,164 + 1,286 = 3,450
5,614 − 2,164 = 3,450
The answers are correct.

Guided Practice

Solve. Use bar models to help you.

1 A computer costs $1,950.
It costs $250 less than a television set.

ⓐ How much does the television set cost?

ⓑ How much do both items cost in all?

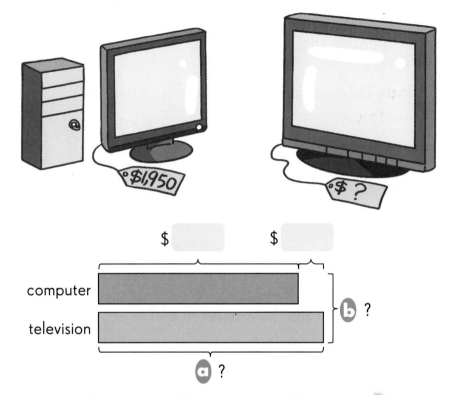

$ [　] 　 $ [　]

computer

television

ⓑ ?

ⓐ ?

ⓐ $ [　] ◯ $ [　] = $ [　]

The television set costs $ [　] .

ⓑ $ [　] ◯ $ [　] = $ [　]

Both items cost $ [　] in all.

The computer costs less than the television set. So, use a comparison model.

2 A school has 720 girls.
It has 250 more boys than girls.
How many children attend the school?

First, find the number
of boys in the school.

3 5,099 passengers are on a cruise ship.
1,825 passengers are children.
How many more adults than children are on the ship?

What do you have
to find first?

4 A farm has 1,263 chicks and hens.
814 of them are chicks.
How many fewer hens than chicks does the shelter have?

Check your
answers.

5 Theater A has 3,460 seats.
Theater B has 290 fewer seats than Theater A.
What is the total number of seats in both theaters?

Let's Explore!

WORK IN PAIRS

STEP 1 Think of two numbers less than 50.

9 and 4 12 and 7

STEP 2 Find the sum and difference of the pair of numbers.

9 + 4 = 13
9 − 4 = 5

12 + 7 = 19
12 − 7 = 5

} **sum**

difference

STEP 3 Add the sum and difference of the pair of numbers.
Compare this with the greater number in the pair.

13 + 5 = 18

19 + 5 = 24

Compare 18 and 9.

Compare 24 and 12.

STEP 4 Repeat **STEP 1** to **STEP 3** with two other pairs of numbers.

STEP 5 Do you see a pattern? Explain your answer.

Let's Practice

Solve. Use bar models to help you.

1 The gymnastic teacher pays $240 for new playground equipment.
The Science teacher pays $85 more for new laboratory equipment.

   a How much does the Science teacher pay?

   b How much do they pay in all?

2 Sarah travels 750 miles.
Quinn travels 125 miles more than Sarah.

   a How many miles does Quinn travel?

   b How many miles do they travel in all?

3 1,235 people attend a dolphin show.
275 fewer people attend a bird show.
How many people attend both shows?

4 Two trucks are carrying a total load of 2,361 oranges.
The first truck carries 886 oranges.
How many more oranges does the second truck
carry than the first truck?

For each bar model, make up a 2-step real-world problem. Then solve.

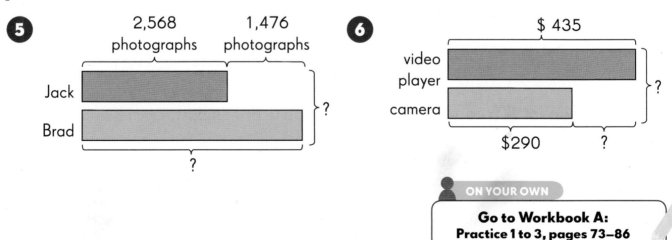

5
2,568 photographs   1,476 photographs

Jack

Brad   ?

?

6
$ 435

video player

camera

$290   ?

?

ON YOUR OWN

Go to Workbook A:
Practice 1 to 3, pages 73–86

Put On Your Thinking Cap!

PROBLEM SOLVING

A farm has 4 kinds of animals and 8 in all.
Some of the animals have 2 legs and some have 4 legs.
The animals have 20 legs altogether.
How many of the animals have 4 legs?
Name the animals that could be under the bushes.

Start by giving 2 legs to each animal.

Remember to add up to 20 legs in all.

_____ of the animals have 4 legs.

The farm animals could be _____ , _____ , _____ , and _____ .

ON YOUR OWN

**Go to Workbook A:
Put on Your Thinking Cap!
pages 87–88**

Chapter Wrap Up

Study Guide
You have learned...

> **Using Bar Models: Addition and Subtraction**

> **Solve 2-step real-world problems**

Addition

a How long is it?

b What is the total length?

a 60 + 10 = 70
Ribbon B is 70 centimeters long.

b 60 + 70 = 130
The total length of ribbons A and B is 130 centimeters.

Subtraction

a Weight? **b** How much less?

a 122 − 80 = 42
The weight of Box B is 42 pounds.

b 80 − 42 = 38
The weight of Box B is 38 pounds less than the weight of Box A.

BIG IDEA

▶ Bar models, addition, and subtraction can be used to solve 2-step real-world problems.

Addition and Subtraction

210 points

June

May

b What is the total score?

a How many points?

80 points

a 210 − 80 = 130
May scored 130 points.

b 210 + 130 = 340
Both girls scored 340 points in all.

Chapter Review/Test

Vocabulary
Choose the correct word.

> bar model
> sum
> difference

1 A [   ] helps you to visualize a problem in pictorial form.

2 The answer to an addition problem is called the [   ].

3 The answer to a subtraction problem is called the [   ].

Concepts and Skills
Find the missing numbers in the bar models.

4

5

6

7

8

9

Problem Solving

Solve. Use bar models to help you.

10 A library has 3,250 fiction books.
It has 1,789 non-fiction books.

 a How many more fiction than non-fiction books does the library have?

 b How many fiction and non-fiction books does the library have in all?

11 315 fans of the home team are at a hockey game.
The visiting team has 28 fewer fans than the home
team at the game.
How many fans are at the game in all?

Chapter 6
Multiplication Tables of 6, 7, 8, and 9

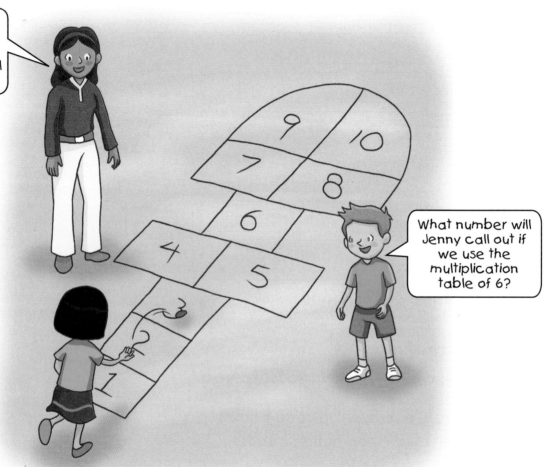

Jenny's marker lands on the number '3'. If we use the multiplication table of 5, Jenny will call out 3 times 5 is '15'.

What number will Jenny call out if we use the multiplication table of 6?

Lessons

BIG IDEA

▶ Many models can be used to multiply.

Multiplication as equal groups

3 twos = 3 groups of 2

4 fives = 4 groups of 5

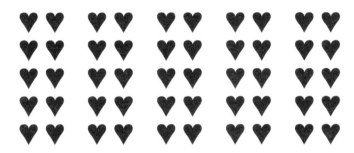

5 tens = 5 groups of 10

Multiplication as repeated addition

2 + 2 + 2 = 6

3 × 2 = 6

4 + 4 + 4 + 4 + 4 = 20

5 × 4 = 20

Multiplying as skip-counting

Skip-counting by 2

0 1 2 3 4 5 6 7 8
Start

4 × 2 = 8

Using multiplication facts you know to find other multiplication facts

6 × 3 = 5 groups of 3 + 1 group of 3
    = 15 + 3
    = 18

8 × 4 = 10 groups of 4 − 2 groups of 4
    = 40 − 8
    = 32

Multiplying numbers in any order

7 × 5 is the same as 5 × 7.
7 × 5 = 35
So, 5 × 7 = 35.

7 × 5

5 × 7

Dividing by sharing equally

Divide 15 circles into 3 equal groups.
How many circles does each group have?

15 ÷ 3 = 5

Each group has 5 circles.

Dividing by grouping

Divide 12 circles into groups so that each group has 2 circles.
How many groups are there?

$12 \div 2 = 6$

There are 6 groups.

Dividing using related multiplication facts

$50 \div 5 = ?$

$10 \times 5 = 50$

So, $50 \div 5 = 10$.

Multiplying and dividing in real-world problems

1 Howard arranges 4 chairs in a row. There are 9 rows.
How many chairs are there in all?

$9 \times 4 = 36$

There are 36 chairs in all.

2 Shelly cooks 24 eggs. She puts 3 eggs on each plate.
How many plates does she use?

$24 \div 3 = 8$

She uses 8 plates.

Find the missing numbers.

1

4 twos = [ ] groups of [ ]

2

[ ] + [ ] + [ ] + [ ] + [ ] = [ ] × 2

= [ ]

Skip-count. Find the missing numbers.

3

[ ] [ ] 9 12 [ ] [ ] 21 24 [ ] [ ]

Find the missing numbers.

4 8 × 2 = 10 groups of 2 − [ ] groups of 2

= [ ] − [ ]

= [ ]

5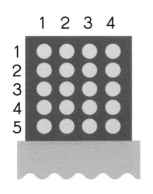

$$\boxed{} \times \boxed{} = 5 \times 4$$

$$= \boxed{}$$

6 $15 \div 3 = ?$

$$\boxed{} \times 3 = 15$$

So, $15 \div 3 = \boxed{}$.

7 $36 \div 4 = ?$

$$\boxed{} \times 4 = 36$$

So, $36 \div 4 = \boxed{}$.

Solve.

8 Angie has 10 pretzels. She puts them equally into 2 bags. How many pretzels does each bag contain?

9 There are 20 students. A van can seat 10 students. How many vans does Mrs. Smith need if she wants to take all the students to the park?

10 Sheena has 9 display cases in her shop. She puts 10 scarves in each case. How many scarves does Sheena have?

11 Andrew has 10 students. He gives 5 tennis balls to each student. How many tennis balls does he give away?

Lesson 6.1 Multiplication Properties

Lesson Objective

- Use multiplication properties.

Learn Use number lines to multiply.

This **number line** shows 1 skip of 3.

skip

```
0   1   2   3
```

The number line shows 1 group of 3 = 1 × 3
                                    = 3.

1 skip of 3 shows
1 group of 3.

This number line shows 2 skips of 3.

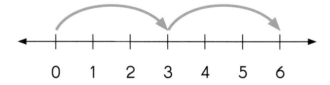

```
0   1   2   3   4   5   6
```

The number line shows 2 groups of 3 = 2 × 3
                                     = 6.

On a number line that shows a multiplication
fact, the skips show the number of equal groups.

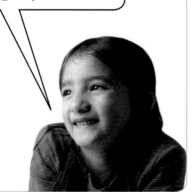

2 skips of 3 shows
2 groups of 3.

Guided Practice

Look at each number line. Express as a multiplication fact.

1

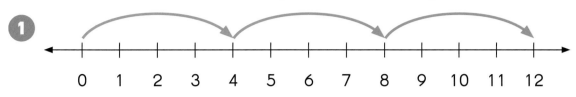

0 1 2 3 4 5 6 7 8 9 10 11 12

[ ] × [ ] = [ ]

2

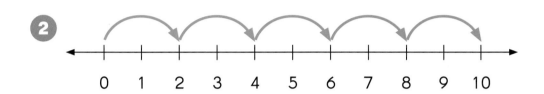

0 1 2 3 4 5 6 7 8 9 10

[ ] × [ ] = [ ]

Express the multiplication fact on each number line.

3 6 × 2 = 12

0 1 2 3 4 5 6 7 8 9 10 11 12

4 3 × 5 = 15

0 1 2 3 4 5 6 7 8 9 10 11 12 13 14 15

Let's Explore!

WORK IN PAIRS

Show two multiplication facts that equal 24.
Use number lines to help you.

Example

8 × 3 = 24

0 1 2 3 4 5 6 7 8 9 10 11 12 13 14 15 16 17 18 19 20 21 22 23 24

1 × ☐ = 24

0 1 2 3 4 5 6 7 8 9 10 11 12 13 14 15 16 17 18 19 20 21 22 23 24

2 × ☐ = 24

0 1 2 3 4 5 6 7 8 9 10 11 12 13 14 15 16 17 18 19 20 21 22 23 24

Numbers can be multiplied in any order.

Using **dot paper**.

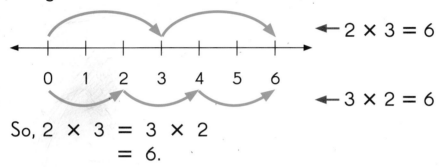

2 groups of 3 or 2 ✕ 3   3 groups of 2 or 3 ✕ 2

Using a number line.

← 2 ✕ 3 = 6

0   1   2   3   4   5   6

← 3 ✕ 2 = 6

So, 2 ✕ 3 = 3 ✕ 2
        = 6.

Changing the order of numbers in a multiplication sentence does not change the answer. This is called the **commutative property** of multiplication.

Guided Practice

Find the missing numbers.

5 6 ✕ 3 = [____]   So, 3 ✕ [____] = [____] .

6 8 ✕ 5 = [____]   So, 5 ✕ [____] = [____] .

Show 5 ✕ 3 = 15 and 3 ✕ 5 = 15. Use the number line provided.

7

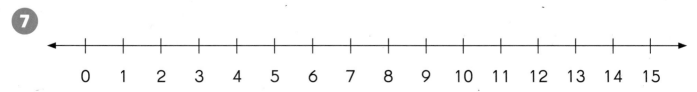

0   1   2   3   4   5   6   7   8   9   10   11   12   13   14   15

Multiply by 1.

Using dot paper.

1
1
2
3

1
1
2
3
4

3 groups of 1 or 3 × 1

4 groups of 1 or 4 × 1

Using a number line.

0   1   2   3

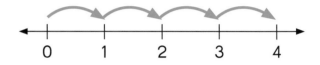

0   1   2   3   4

3 groups of 1

3 × 1 = 3

4 groups of 1

4 × 1 = 4

1 × 3 = 3
3 × 1 = 3
So, 1 × 3 = 3 × 1.

1 × 4 = 4
4 × 1 = 4
So, 1 × 4 = 4 × 1.

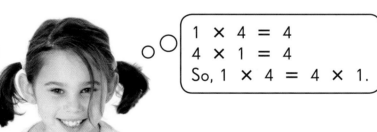

Any number multiplied by 1 equals that number.
This is called the **multiplicative property of one**.

Guided Practice

Look at each number line. Express as a multiplication fact.

8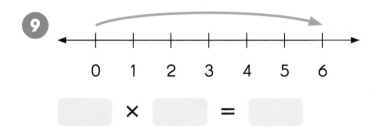

0   1   2   3   4   5   6

[ ] × [ ] = [ ]

9

0   1   2   3   4   5   6

[ ] × [ ] = [ ]

10 So, 1 × 6 = 6 × [ ].

= [ ]

Find the missing numbers.

11

1 × [ ] = 5

5 × [ ] = [ ]

Complete the multiplication sentences. Use the numbers provided.

12 [ ] × [ ] = [ ]

13 [ ] × [ ] = [ ]

Learn **Multiply by 0.**

There are 4 empty plates, which means there are 4 groups of nothing.

So, 4 × 0 = 0.

4 × 0 = 0
So, 0 × 4 = 0.

Any number multiplied by 0 equals 0.
This is called the **multiplicative property of zero**.

Guided Practice

Find the missing numbers.

14

[ ] × [ ] = [ ]

[ ] × [ ] = [ ]

Find the missing numbers.

15 0 × ⬜ = ⬜

16 ⬜ × ⬜ = 0

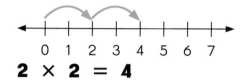 **Numbers can be grouped and multiplied in any order.**

2 × 2 × 5 = ?

Method 1

Step 1 Multiply the first two numbers.

0 1 2 3 4 5 6 7

2 × 2 = 4

Step 2 Multiply the last number by the answer in Step 1.

0 1 2 3 4 5 6 7 8 9 10 11 12 13 14 15 16 17 18 19 20

4 × 5 = 20

So, **2** × **2** × 5 = **4** × 5

= 20.

Continued on next page

$2 \times 2 \times 5 = ?$

Method 2

Step 1   Multiply the last two numbers.

$2 \times 5 = 10$

Step 2   Multiply the first number by the answer in Step 1.

$2 \times 10 = 20$

So, $2 \times 2 \times 5 = 2 \times 10$
$= 20.$

What do you notice about your answers?

$2 \times 2 \times 5 = 20$

$2 \times 2 \times 5 = 20$

In both methods, you get the same answer.

Changing the way numbers in a multiplication sentence are grouped and multiplied does not change the answer. This is called the **associative property** of multiplication.

Multiply. Use the number lines provided.

17 5 × 2 × 3 = ?

Method 1
Step 1 Multiply the first two numbers.

[ ] × [ ] = [ ]

Step 2 Multiply the last number by the answer in Step 1.

[ ] × [ ] = [ ]

So, **5** × **2** × 3 = [ ] × [ ]

= [ ] .

Method 2
Step 1 Multiply the last two numbers.

[ ] × [ ] = [ ]

Step 2 Multiply the first number by the answer in Step 1.

[ ] × [ ] = [ ]

So, 5 × **2** × **3** = [ ] × [ ]

= [ ] .

Complete.

Find the missing numbers. Use the answers from Exercise 17 on page 147.

(18) [ ] × [ ] × [ ] = [ ] × [ ] × [ ]

[ ] × [ ] = [ ] × [ ]

= [ ]

(19) 4 × 2 × 2 = ?

Method 1

Step 1   4 × 2 = [ ]

Step 2   [ ] × 2 = [ ]

Method 2

Step 1   2 × 2 = [ ]

Step 2   4 × [ ] = [ ]

So, 4 × 2 × 2 = [ ] .

Find the missing numbers.

(20) 8 × 7 = [ ] × 2 × 7

(21) 5 × 6 = 5 × 3 × [ ]

(22) [ ] × 3 × [ ] = 18

(23) 2 × [ ] × [ ] = 32

Let's Practice

Complete each multiplication fact. Then show on each number line.

1 3 × 3 = [ ]

```
0   1   2   3   4   5   6   7   8   9   10  11  12
```

2 5 × 2 = [ ]

```
0   1   2   3   4   5   6   7   8   9   10  11  12
```

Look at each number line. Then express as a multiplication fact.

3

```
0 1 2 3 4 5 6 7 8 9 10 11 12 13 14 15 16 17 18
```

[ ] × [ ] = [ ]

4

```
0 1 2 3 4 5 6 7 8 9 10 11 12 13 14 15 16 17 18
```

[ ] × [ ] = [ ]

Lesson 6.1 Multiplication Properties   **149**

Find the missing numbers.

5 $5 \times \boxed{} = \boxed{} \times 5$
$\phantom{5 \times \boxed{00}} = 5$

6 $\boxed{} \times 1 = 1 \times \boxed{}$
$\phantom{\boxed{00} \times 1} = 8$

7 $\boxed{} \times 7 = 7 \times \boxed{}$
$\phantom{\boxed{00} \times 7} = 0$

8 $6 \times 0 = \boxed{} \times 6$
$ = \boxed{}$

9 $2 \times 2 \times 3 = \boxed{} \times \boxed{}$
$ = \boxed{}$

10 $12 \times 3 = \boxed{} \times 6 \times 3$

11 $3 \times 8 = 3 \times 2 \times \boxed{}$

ON YOUR OWN

**Go to Workbook A:
Practice 1, pages 93–96**

6.2 Multiply by 6

Lesson Objectives

- Understand multiplication by using array models.
- Practice multiplication facts of 6.

Vocabulary
array model

Learn Use array models to show multiplication facts.

Jasper cuts out 5 shapes.
He counts the number of sides on each shape.
There are 6 sides on each shape.
What is the total number of sides of all 5 shapes?

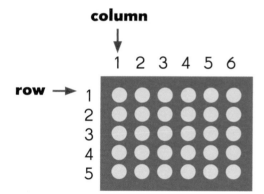

column
↓
1 2 3 4 5 6

row →

This is an array model.

There are 5 rows of 6 dots.

$$5 \times 6 = 6 \times 5$$
$$= 30$$

The total number of sides is 30.

$5 \times 6 = ?$
5 rows of 6 = 30

$6 \times 5 = ?$
6 fives = 3 tens
So, $6 \times 5 = 30$.

A dot paper is an **array model**.
The dots are arranged in rows and columns.
In multiplication, each row has the same number of dots.

Guided Practice

Solve. Use array models to help you.

1 Ricky keeps 10 beetles. Each beetle has 6 legs.
How many legs do the beetles have in all?

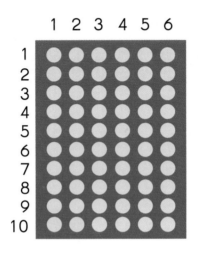

$10 \times 6 = $ ☐ $\times$ ☐

$= $ ☐

The beetles have ☐ legs in all.

2 A flower has 6 petals.
Julia buys 4 flowers.
How many petals does Julia have in all?

$4 \times 6 = $ ☐ $\times$ ☐

$= $ ☐

Julia has ☐ petals in all.

Use multiplication facts you know to find other multiplication facts.

$7 \times 6 = ?$

Start with 5 groups of 6.

1 2 3 4 5 6

$5 \times 6 = 30$

$7 \times 6 =$ 5 groups of 6
$\quad\quad\quad\quad + $ 2 groups of 6
$\quad\quad = 30 + 12$
$\quad\quad = 42$

7 × 6 is the same as adding 2 groups of 6 to 5 groups of 6.

5 × 6 = 6 × 5
$\quad\quad = 30$

Continued on next page

$9 \times 6 = ?$

Start with 10 groups of 6.

$10 \times 6 = 60$

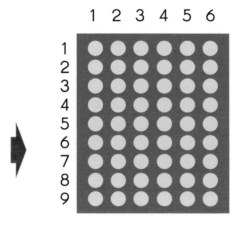

$9 \times 6 = 10$ groups of 6
$ - 1$ group of 6
$ = 60 - 6$
$ = 54$

$10 \times 6 = 6 \times 10$
$ = 60$

9×6 is the same as subtracting 1 group of 6 from 10×6.

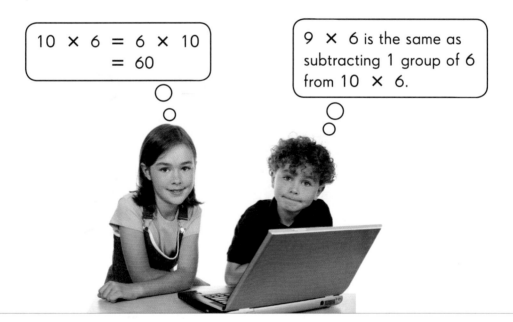

Guided Practice

Find the missing numbers. Use array models to help you.

3 6 × 6 = ?

Start with 5 groups of 6.

5 × 6 = [   ]

6 × 6 = 5 groups of 6

      + [   ] group of 6

    = 30 + [   ]

    = [   ]

4 8 × 6 = ?

Start with 10 groups of 6.

10 × 6 = [   ]

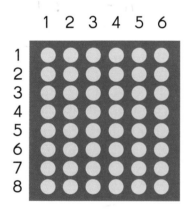

8 × 6 = 10 groups of 6

     − [   ] groups of 6

   = 60 − [   ]

   = [   ]

WORKING TOGETHER ▶ **Game**

Number Train!

Each player gets a number train as shown.

STEP 1 Player 1 chooses a face-up number card, such as 2.

STEP 2 Player 1 then rolls the number cube to get another number, such as number 6.
Player 1 then multiplies the two numbers.
$2 \times 6 = 12$
The other players check the answer.

STEP 3 If Player 1's answer is correct, he or she colors the answer on his or her number train.
If the answer is correct but not on the train, roll a second time.
If the second answer is still not on the train, the game moves on to the next player.

STEP 4 Players take turns. A player gets one bonus roll with each completely colored car.

The first player to color all the numbers on the train wins!

Multiplication Table of 6

1	×	6	=	6
2	×	6	=	12
3	×	6	=	18
4	×	6	=	24
5	×	6	=	30
6	×	6	=	36
7	×	6	=	42
8	×	6	=	48
9	×	6	=	54
10	×	6	=	60

Let's Practice

Complete each skip-counting pattern.

1. 6   12   18   ☐   ☐   ☐

2. 24   30   36   ☐   ☐   ☐

Multiply. Use array models to help you.

3. $5 \times 6 = $ ☐

4. $6 \times 6 = $ ☐

5. $7 \times 6 = $ ☐

6. $8 \times 6 = $ ☐

7. $9 \times 6 = $ ☐

8. $10 \times 6 = $ ☐

9. $3 \times 6 = $ ☐

10. $5 \times 6 = $ ☐

ON YOUR OWN

Go to Workbook A:
Practice 2, pages 97–100

Lesson 6.3 Multiply by 7

Lesson Objectives

- Understand multiplication by using area models.
- Practice multiplication facts of 7.

Learn **Use area models to show multiplication facts.**

Tracy has some craft sticks.
She makes 4 similar shapes with them.
She uses 7 craft sticks for each shape.

How many craft sticks does she use in all?

This is an **area model**.

$4 \times 7 = ?$

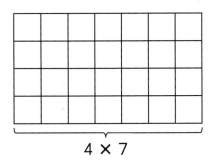

4×7

$$4 \times 7 = 7 + 7 + 7 + 7$$
$$ = 28$$

4 rows of 7
$= 7 + 7 + 7 + 7$

She uses 28 craft sticks in all.

Guided Practice

Solve. Use area models to help you.

1 Jen has 3 pea pods.
Each pea pod contains 7 peas.
How many peas does Jen have in all?

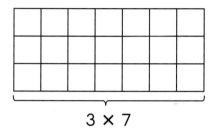

3 × 7

☐ × ☐ = ☐ + ☐ + ☐

= ☐

Jen has ☐ peas in all.

2 Allyson has 5 bracelets.
Each bracelet has 7 beads.
How many beads does Allyson have in all?

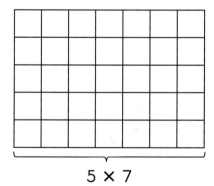

5 × 7

☐ × ☐ = ☐ + ☐ + ☐ + ☐ + ☐

= ☐

Allyson has ☐ beads in all.

Use multiplication facts you know to find other multiplication facts.

$6 \times 7 = ?$
Start with 5 groups of 7.

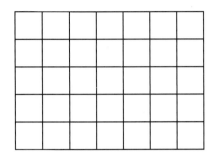

$5 \times 7 = 35$

$6 \times 7 = 5$ groups of $7 + 1$ group of 7
$\qquad = 35 + 7$
$\qquad = 42$

$5 \times 7 = 7 \times 5$
$\qquad = 35$

6×7 is the same as adding 1 group of 7 to 5×7.

$10 \times 7 = 7 \times 10$
$\qquad = 70$

9×7 is the same as subtracting 1 group of 7 from 10×7.

$9 \times 7 = ?$
Start with 10 groups of 7.

$10 \times 7 = 70$

$9 \times 7 = 10$ groups of $7 - 1$ group of 7
$\qquad = 70 - 7$
$\qquad = 63$

Guided Practice

Find the missing numbers. Use area models to help you.

3 7 × 7 = ?
Start with 5 groups of 7.

  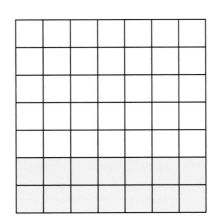

5 × 7 = [ ]

7 × 7 = 5 groups of 7 + [ ] groups of 7

= 35 + [ ]

= [ ]

4 8 × 7 = ?
Start with 10 groups of 7.

  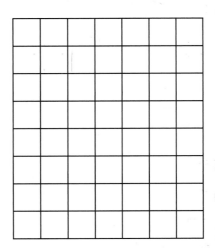

10 × 7 = [ ]

8 × 7 = 10 groups of 7 − [ ] groups of 7

= [ ] − [ ]

= [ ]

Multiplication Table of 7

1	×	7	=	7
2	×	7	=	14
3	×	7	=	21
4	×	7	=	28
5	×	7	=	35
6	×	7	=	42
7	×	7	=	49
8	×	7	=	56
9	×	7	=	63
10	×	7	=	70

Let's Practice

Complete each skip-counting pattern.

1. 7   14   21   ___   ___   ___

2. 28   35   42   ___   ___   ___

Multiply.

3. 4 × 7 = ___

4. 5 × 7 = ___

5. 6 × 7 = ___

6. 8 × 7 = ___

7. 9 × 7 = ___

8. 10 × 7 = ___

ON YOUR OWN

Go to Workbook A:
Practice 3, pages 101–104

Lesson 6.4 Multiply by 8

Lesson Objectives

- Understand multiplication by using number lines and area models.
- Practice multiplication facts of 8.

Learn **Use number lines to show multiplication facts.**

At the aquarium, Hector sees 3 octopuses.
Each octopus has 8 tentacles.
How many tentacles do the octopuses have in all?

3 groups of 8 legs
= 3 × 8

0   8   16   24

3 skips of 8 show 3 groups of 8.

So, 3 × 8 = 24.

I can also show 3 × 8
in another way.
8 groups of 3 = 8 × 3

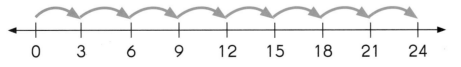

0 3 6 9 12 15 18 21 24

8 skips of 3 show 8 groups of 3.

So, 8 × 3 = 24.

Guided Practice

Look at the number line. Then express as a multiplication fact.

1

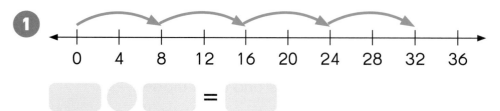

0   4   8   12   16   20   24   28   32   36

☐ ⬤ ☐ = ☐

Express the multiplication fact on the number line. Then complete.

2

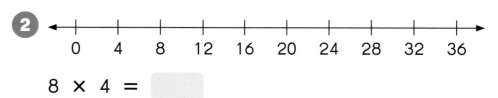

0   4   8   12   16   20   24   28   32   36

8 × 4 = ☐

Learn Use multiplication facts you know to find other multiplication facts.

Kathy has 6 spiders. Each spider has 8 legs.
How many legs do the spiders have in all.

5 × 8 { ... } 6 × 8

6 × 8 = 5 groups of 8 + 1 group of 8
    = 40 + 8
    = 48

The spiders have 48 legs
in all.

```
5 × 8 = 8 × 5
      = 40
6 × 8 is the same as adding
1 group of 8 to 5 × 8.
```

Guided Practice

Solve. Use area models to help you.

3 Lily has 7 packs of paper plates.
Each pack contains 8 paper plates.
How many paper plates does Lily have in all?

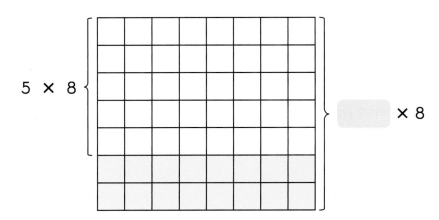

5×8

$\boxed{} \times 8$

$7 \times 8 = 5$ groups of $8 + \boxed{}$ groups of 8

$\qquad = 40 + \boxed{}$

$\qquad = \boxed{}$

Lily has $\boxed{}$ paper plates in all.

$5 \times 8 = 8 \times 5$
$\qquad\quad = 40$
7×8 is the same as
adding 2 groups of 8
to 5×8.

Game

Let's Multiply!

Players: **4 to 6**
Materials:
- worksheets
- digit cards with numbers from 1 to 9
- multiplier cards with numbers from 6 to 8

Each player uses the worksheet provided.

×	1	2	3	4	5	6	7	8	9
8									
7									
6									

STEP 1 Player 1 draws a digit card and a multiplier card.

STEP 2 Player 1 multiplies the number on the digit card by the number on the multiplier card. The other players check the answer.

$6 \times 8 = 48$

STEP 3 Player 1 writes the answer in the correct box on the worksheet.
The player does not write on the worksheet if the answer is incorrect.

STEP 4 Return the cards and mix them up. Players take turns to play.

The first player to fill a complete row on the worksheet wins!

Multiplication Table of 8

1	×	8	=	8
2	×	8	=	16
3	×	8	=	24
4	×	8	=	32
5	×	8	=	40
6	×	8	=	48
7	×	8	=	56
8	×	8	=	64
9	×	8	=	72
10	×	8	=	80

Let's Practice

Complete each skip-counting pattern.

1 8 16 24

2 32 40 48

Multiply.

3 6 × 8 =

4 7 × 8 =

5 9 × 8 =

6 10 × 8 =

ON YOUR OWN

**Go to Workbook A:
Practice 4, pages 105–108**

Lesson 6.5 Multiply by 9

Lesson Objectives

* Understand multiplication by using array models and area models.
* Practice multiplication facts of 9.

Learn · Use array models to show multiplication facts.

Serena bundles 9 straws into one group.
She bundles 3 groups of straws.
How many straws does she have in all?

Look at the array models.

```
  1 2 3 4 5 6 7 8 9
1 ● ● ● ● ● ● ● ● ●
2 ● ● ● ● ● ● ● ● ●
3 ● ● ● ● ● ● ● ● ●
```

3 groups of 9 straws
= 3 × 9

```
  1 2 3
1 ● ● ●
2 ● ● ●
3 ● ● ●
4 ● ● ●
5 ● ● ●
6 ● ● ●
7 ● ● ●
8 ● ● ●
9 ● ● ●
```

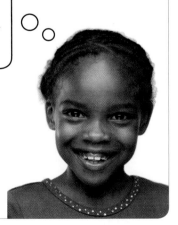

3 × 9 = 9 × 3
I can also show the array
as 9 × 3.

9 × 3 = 27
So, 3 × 9 = 27.
She has 27 straws in all.

Guided Practice

Look at the array model. Then express as a multiplication fact.

1

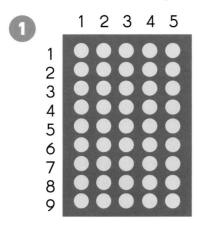

$$\boxed{} \;\bullet\; \boxed{} = \boxed{}$$

Show 5 × 9 on the array model. Then express as a multiplication fact.

2

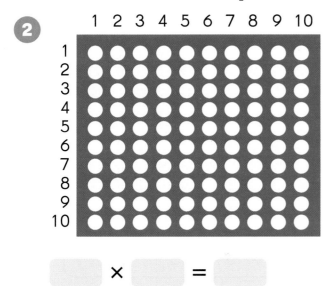

$$\boxed{} \times \boxed{} = \boxed{}$$

Use area models and multiplication facts you know to find other multiplication facts.

Learn

$4 \times 9 = ?$

$4 \times 9 = 9 \times 4$

10×4 { } 9×4

$4 \times 9 = 9 \times 4$
I can show the area model as 9×4.
$9 \times 4 = 36$

9×4 is the same as subtracting 1 group of 4 from 10×4.

$9 \times 4 = 10$ groups of $4 - 1$ group of 4
$ = 40 - 4$
$ = 36$

So, $4 \times 9 = 36$.

$5 \times 9 = ?$

$5 \times 9 = 9 \times 5$

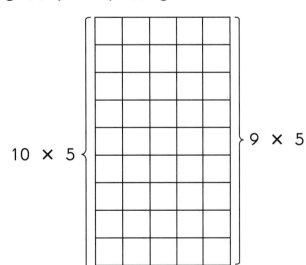

10×5 { 9×5

$5 \times 9 = 9 \times 5$
I can show the area model as 9×5.
$9 \times 5 = 45$

$9 \times 5 = 10$ groups of $5 - 1$ group of 5
$\qquad = 50 - 5$
$\qquad = 45$

So, $5 \times 9 = 45$.

Do you see a pattern?

9 times any number is 10 times the number minus the number.

Guided Practice

Solve. Use area models to help you.

3 $6 \times 9 = ?$

$6 \times 9 = 9 \times 6$

$9 \times 6 = 10$ groups of $6 - \boxed{}$ group of 6

$\qquad = 60 - \boxed{}$

$\qquad = \boxed{}$

So, $6 \times 9 = \boxed{}$.

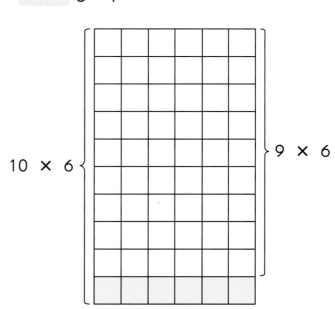

Solve.

4 Mr. Leeson has 8 mirrors.
Each mirror has 9 sides.
How many sides do the mirrors have in all?

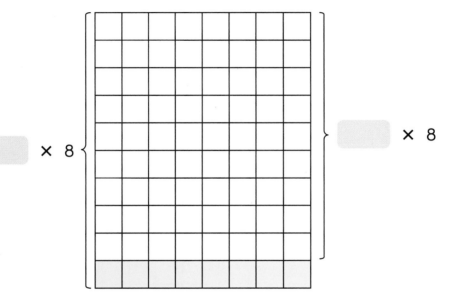

8 × 9 = 9 × 8

9 × 8 = 10 groups of 8 − [ ] group of 8

= 80 − [ ]

= [ ]

8 mirrors have [ ] sides in all.

Use finger counting to show multiplication facts of 9.

$1 \times 9 = 9$

9

$1 \times 9 = 9$

$2 \times 9 = 18$

1   **8**

$2 \times 9 = 18$

$3 \times 9 = 27$

2   **7**

$3 \times 9 = 27$

I bend my third finger to show 3 times 9.
$3 \times 9 = 27$

Guided Practice

Multiply. Use finger counting.

5 $5 \times 9 =$

6 $9 \times 9 =$

Get to the Top!

Players: 4
Materials:
- question cards with multiplication facts of 6, 7, 8, and 9
- number board
- 8 counters for each player

Each player chooses one path on the number board.

STEP 1 Each player places a counter on the first empty space of his or her path.

STEP 2 Player 1 draws a question card and answers the question.
For example, 5 × 6 = 30
The other players check the answer.

STEP 3 Player 1 places a counter on the answer if it is on his or her path.

If the answer is not on Player 1's path or if the answer is wrong, Player 1 does not place any counter on the number board.

STEP 4 Players take turns. Players do not return the cards to the stack after each play.

The first player to reach the top by completely covering the path with counters wins!

Multiplication Table of 9

1	×	9	=	9
2	×	9	=	18
3	×	9	=	27
4	×	9	=	36
5	×	9	=	45
6	×	9	=	54
7	×	9	=	63
8	×	9	=	72
9	×	9	=	81
10	×	9	=	90

Let's Practice

Complete each skip-counting pattern.

1 9 18 27

2 36 45 54

Multiply. Use any method.

3 $2 \times 9 =$

4 $7 \times 9 =$

5 $5 \times 9 =$

6 $4 \times 9 =$

7 $6 \times 9 =$

8 $3 \times 9 =$

ON YOUR OWN

Go to Workbook A:
Practice 5, pages 109–112

Division: Finding the Number of Items in Each Group

Lesson Objectives

- Divide to find the number of items in each group.
- Understand related multiplication and division facts.
- Write division sentences for real-world problems.

Vocabulary
equal groups

Learn **Divide to find the number of items in each group by using related multiplication facts.**

Divide 42 cubes into 6 **equal groups**.
How many cubes does each group have?

Think of a related multiplication fact.

6 × 7 = 42
So, 42 ÷ 6 = 7.

Each group has 7 cubes.

Guided Practice

Solve. Use related multiplication facts to help you.

1 Divide 48 marbles into 8 equal groups.
How many marbles does each group have?

$8 \times 6 = 48$

So, $48 \div 8 = \boxed{}$.

Each group has $\boxed{}$ marbles.

Think of a related multiplication fact.

2 Divide 35 glasses equally among 7 trays.
How many glasses does each tray have?

Let's Practice

Find the missing numbers.

$8 \times \boxed{} = 56$ So, $56 \div 8 = \boxed{}$.

$7 \times \boxed{} = 49$ So, $49 \div 7 = \boxed{}$.

Express two division sentences for each multiplication sentence.

3 $9 \times 4 = 36$

4 $5 \times 7 = 35$

Solve. Use related multiplication facts to help you.

5 Divide 48 beads into 8 equal containers.
How many beads does each container have?

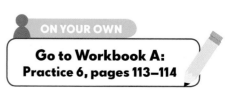

ON YOUR OWN

Go to Workbook A:
Practice 6, pages 113–114

6.7 Division: Making Equal Groups

Lesson Objectives

- Divide to find the number of groups.
- Understand related multiplication and division facts.
- Express division sentences for real-world problems.

Learn ## Divide to make equal groups by using related multiplication facts.

Divide 56 stars into equal groups.
Each group has 8 stars.
How many groups are formed?

Think of a related multiplication fact.

$7 \times 8 = 56$

So, $56 \div 8 = 7$.

7 groups are formed.

Guided Practice

Solve. Use related multiplication facts to help you.

1 Divide 54 crackers into equal plates of 6 crackers.
How many plates are needed?

[   ] × 6 = 54

So, 54 ÷ 6 = [   ].

[   ] plates are needed.

> Think of a related multiplication fact.

2 Jim packs 63 pencils into some boxes equally.
Each box contains 9 pencils.
How many boxes does Jim use?

 Hands-On Activity

WORK IN PAIRS

Tell a division story by arranging objects into groups of 6, 7, 8, or 9.
Have a classmate solve it.

Example

Benny has to store 36 stuffed animals in boxes.
He puts 9 stuffed animals in each box.

How many boxes does Benny use?

36 ÷ 9 = 4

Benny uses 4 boxes.

Let's Practice

Find the missing numbers.

1 ☐ × 7 = 28

So, 28 ÷ 7 = ☐.

2 ☐ × 8 = 48

So, 48 ÷ 8 = ☐.

Express two division sentences for each multiplication sentence.

3 6 × 9 = 54

4 7 × 6 = 42

Divide. Use related multiplication facts to help you.

5 36 ÷ 6 = ☐

6 63 ÷ 7 = ☐

7 40 ÷ 8 = ☐

8 72 ÷ 9 = ☐

Solve. Use related multiplication facts to help you.

9 Betty puts 9 raisins in a muffin.
She uses 45 raisins in all.
How many muffins does she puts raisins in?

10 Shona collects 32 leaves.
She pastes 8 leaves on each page of her scrapbook.
How many pages of her scrapbook does she fill?

ON YOUR OWN

Go to Workbook A:
Practice 7, page 115

Put On Your Thinking Cap!

PROBLEM SOLVING

Find the numbers.

Example

I have a number.
When I multiply the number by 9, the answer is 72.
What is my number?

I divide 72 by 9.
$72 \div 9 = 8$

My number is 8.

I can work backward to find the answer.

I divide because it is the opposite of multiplying.

1. I have two numbers.
   When I multiply each number by 8, the answers will both be less than 60 but greater than 45.
   What are my numbers?

2. Make up your own multiplication or division riddle and have a classmate solve it.

ON YOUR OWN

**Go to Workbook A:
Put on Your Thinking Cap!
pages 117–118**

Chapter Wrap Up

Study Guide
You have learned...

Multiplication Tables of 6, 7, 8, and 9

Multiplication Properties

Commutative Property

Changing the order of numbers in a multiplication sentence does not change the answer.

Example

$4 \times 5 = 20$
$5 \times 4 = 20$

So, $4 \times 5 = 5 \times 4$
$\qquad = 20.$

Multiplicative Property of One

Any number multiplied by 1 equals that number.

Example

$1 \times 6 = 6$
$6 \times 1 = 6$

$1 \times 9 = 9$
$9 \times 1 = 9$

Multiplicative Property of Zero

Any number multiplied by 0 equals 0.

Example

$5 \times 0 = 0$
$0 \times 5 = 0$

$8 \times 0 = 0$
$0 \times 8 = 0$

Associative Property

Changing the way numbers in a multiplication sentence are grouped and multiplied does not change the answer.

Example

$\mathbf{2 \times 3} \times 3 = \mathbf{6} \times 3$
$\qquad\qquad = 18$
$2 \times \mathbf{3 \times 3} = 2 \times \mathbf{9}$
$\qquad\qquad = \mathbf{18}$

In both methods, you get the same answer.

BIG IDEA
► Many models can be used to multiply.

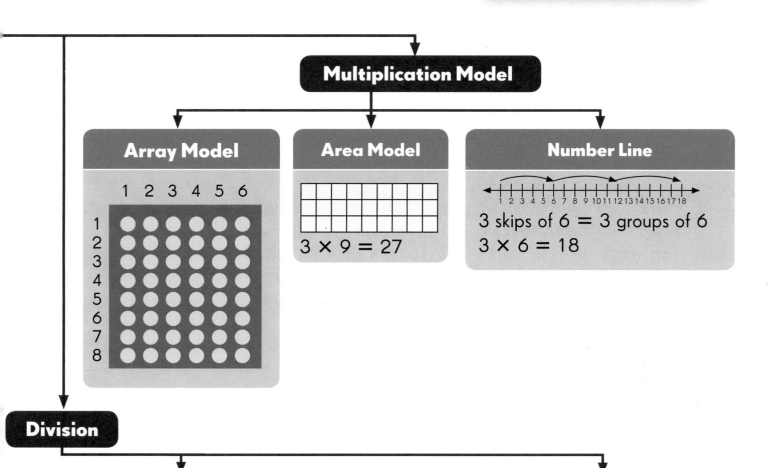

Multiplication Model

Array Model

1 2 3 4 5 6

1
2
3
4
5
6
7
8

Area Model

3 × 9 = 27

Number Line

1 2 3 4 5 6 7 8 9 10 11 12 13 14 15 16 17 18
3 skips of 6 = 3 groups of 6
3 × 6 = 18

Division

Dividing to Find the Number of Items in Each Group

Julie divides 56 flowers equally into 7 vases. How many flowers does each vase hold?

7 × 8 = 56

56 ÷ 7 = 8

Each vase holds 8 flowers.

Dividing to Make Equal Groups

Abel divides 36 footballs into equal groups. There are 9 footballs in each group. How many groups of football does Abel form?

4 × 9 = 36

36 ÷ 9 = 4

Abel forms 4 groups of footballs.

Chapter Review/Test

Vocabulary
Choose the correct word.

| commutative |
| associative |
| array |
| division |
| skips |
| equal |

1 When using a number line to multiply, the number of _____ shows the number of equal groups.

2 When items are divided into _____ groups, the number of items in each group is the same.

3 The _____ property states that changing the order of numbers in a multiplication sentence does not change the answer.

4 The _____ property states that changing the way numbers in a multiplication sentence are grouped and multiplied does not change the answer.

Concepts and Skills
Find the array model that shows 2 × 5.

5

Ⓐ

Ⓑ

Ⓒ

Find the missing number. Choose the correct area model.

6 7 × 9 = [ ]

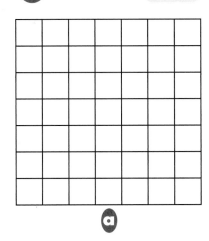

ⓐ

ⓑ

Express the multiplication fact in Exercise 6 another way. Choose the correct area model.

7 [ ] × [ ] = [ ]

ⓐ

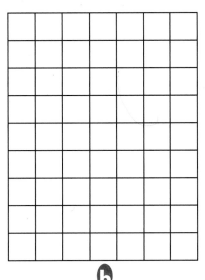

ⓑ

Look at the number line. Then express as a multiplication fact.

8

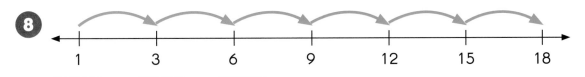

| 1 | 3 | 6 | 9 | 12 | 15 | 18 |

[ ] × [ ] = [ ]

Express the multiplication sentence in Exercise 8 in another way. Use the number line provided.

9

[ ] × [ ] = [ ]

Multiply.

10 2 × 6 = [ ]

11 3 × 7 = [ ]

12 5 × 9 = [ ]

13 5 × 8 = [ ]

14 6 × 7 = [ ]

15 8 × 1 = [ ]

16 0 × 5 = [ ]

17 10 × 9 = [ ]

Find the missing numbers.

18 5 × 1 × 9 = [ ] × 9

= [ ]

19 8 × 5 × 2 = 8 × [ ]

= [ ]

20 5 × 6 = [ ]

[ ] ÷ 6 = 5

21 7 × [ ] = 28

28 ÷ 7 = [ ]

22 [ ] × 9 = 72

72 ÷ 9 = [ ]

23 80 ÷ [ ] = 8

[ ] × 8 = 80

Problem Solving
Solve.

24 Mr. Johnson owns 7 cats. Each cat has 6 kittens. How many kittens does Mr. Johnson own?

25 Martin has 81 sheep. He divides his sheep equally into 9 pens. How many sheep are put in each pen?

26 Ellen has 63 cherries. She puts 7 cherries into each bowl. How many bowls does she use?

7 Multiplication

Let's Have Fun With Spiders!

Ingredients:
pretzel
crackers
honey
raisins

Body: Use crackers.

Legs: Use eight 6-centimeter pieces of pretzel. Stick four pieces to each side of the crackers with honey.

Eyes: Use two small raisins. Stick each of them on top of the cracker with honey.

Break each pretzel to make the legs look jointed.

How many legs does a spider have? I want to make 5 spiders. How many pieces of pretzel do I need for the legs?

Lessons

BIG IDEAS

▶ Mental math can be used to multiply.
▶ Numbers up to 3-digits can be multiplied with or without regrouping.

Recall Prior Knowledge

Multiplication as repeated addition

$7 + 7 + 7 + 7 + 7 + 7 = 42$
$6 \times 7 = 42$

$10 + 10 + 10 = 30$
$3 \times 10 = 30$

Multiplication as skip-counting

Skip-counting by 3

0 1 2 3 4 5 6 7 8 9 10 11 12
Start

$4 \times 3 = 12$

Multiplication tables of 2, 3, 4, and 5

$1 \times 2 = 2$	$1 \times 3 = 3$	$1 \times 4 = 4$	$1 \times 5 = 5$
$2 \times 2 = 4$	$2 \times 3 = 6$	$2 \times 4 = 8$	$2 \times 5 = 10$
$3 \times 2 = 6$	$3 \times 3 = 9$	$3 \times 4 = 12$	$3 \times 5 = 15$
$4 \times 2 = 8$	$4 \times 3 = 12$	$4 \times 4 = 16$	$4 \times 5 = 20$
$5 \times 2 = 10$	$5 \times 3 = 15$	$5 \times 4 = 20$	$5 \times 5 = 25$
$6 \times 2 = 12$	$6 \times 3 = 18$	$6 \times 4 = 24$	$6 \times 5 = 30$
$7 \times 2 = 14$	$7 \times 3 = 21$	$7 \times 4 = 28$	$7 \times 5 = 35$
$8 \times 2 = 16$	$8 \times 3 = 24$	$8 \times 4 = 32$	$8 \times 5 = 40$
$9 \times 2 = 18$	$9 \times 3 = 27$	$9 \times 4 = 36$	$9 \times 5 = 45$
$10 \times 2 = 20$	$10 \times 3 = 30$	$10 \times 4 = 40$	$10 \times 5 = 50$

Multiplication tables of 6, 7, 8, 9, and 10

1 × 6 = 6	1 × 7 = 7	1 × 8 = 8	1 × 9 = 9	1 × 10 = 10
2 × 6 = 12	2 × 7 = 14	2 × 8 = 16	2 × 9 = 18	2 × 10 = 20
3 × 6 = 18	3 × 7 = 21	3 × 8 = 24	3 × 9 = 27	3 × 10 = 30
4 × 6 = 24	4 × 7 = 28	4 × 8 = 32	4 × 9 = 36	4 × 10 = 40
5 × 6 = 30	5 × 7 = 35	5 × 8 = 40	5 × 9 = 45	5 × 10 = 50
6 × 6 = 36	6 × 7 = 42	6 × 8 = 48	6 × 9 = 54	6 × 10 = 60
7 × 6 = 42	7 × 7 = 49	7 × 8 = 56	7 × 9 = 63	7 × 10 = 70
8 × 6 = 48	8 × 7 = 56	8 × 8 = 64	8 × 9 = 72	8 × 10 = 80
9 × 6 = 54	9 × 7 = 63	9 × 8 = 72	9 × 9 = 81	9 × 10 = 90
10 × 6 = 60	10 × 7 = 70	10 × 8 = 80	10 × 9 = 90	10 × 10 = 100

Multiplying numbers in any order

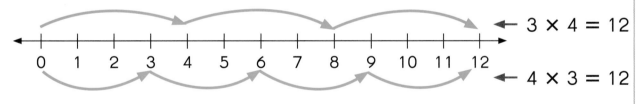

← 3 × 4 = 12

← 4 × 3 = 12

So, 3 × 4 = 4 × 3
          = 12.

Using multiplication facts you know to find other multiplication facts

6 × 7 = 5 groups of 7 + 1 group of 7
      = 35 + 7
      = 42

9 × 7 = 10 groups of 7 − 1 group of 7
      = 70 − 7
      = 63

Recall Prior Knowledge

Multiplying by 0

Any number multiplied by 0 equals 0.
$0 \times 10 = 0$
$4 \times 0 = 0$

Multiplying by 1

Any number multiplied by 1 equals that number.
$1 \times 3 = 3$ $7 \times 1 = 7$

✔ Quick Check

Find the missing numbers.

1 $4 + 4 + 4 + 4 + 4 = \boxed{} \times 4$

$= \boxed{}$

2

5   10 $\boxed{}$ $\boxed{}$ 25   30   35   40 $\boxed{}$ $\boxed{}$

Find the missing numbers.

3 $7 \times 5 = \boxed{}$

So, $5 \times 7 = \boxed{}$.

Find the missing numbers.

4 $7 \times 8 = 5$ groups of $8 + \boxed{}$ groups of 8

$= 40 + \boxed{}$

$= \boxed{}$

5 $8 \times 6 = 10$ groups of $6 - \boxed{}$ groups of 6

$= 60 - \boxed{}$

$= \boxed{}$

Multiply.

6 $7 \times 9 = \boxed{}$ **7** $7 \times 7 = \boxed{}$ **8** $9 \times 6 = \boxed{}$

7.1 Mental Multiplication

Lesson Objective

- Multiply ones, tens, and hundreds mentally.

Learn **Multiply ones mentally.**

Find 4 × 3.

4 × 3 = 12

Find 3 × 4.

3 × 4 = 12

I skip-count by 3s.
3   6   9   12
I skip-count by 4s.
4   8   12
So, 4 × 3 is the
same as 3 × 4.

Guided Practice

Multiply. Find the missing numbers.

1 4 × 6 = ?

6 × 4 =

4 × 6 =

2 8 × 3 = ?

3 × 8 =

8 × 3 =

3 5 × 7 = ?

7 × 5 =

5 × 7 =

4 9 × 10 = ?

10 × 9 =

9 × 10 =

Learn — Multiply by tens or hundreds mentally.

Find 5 × 40.
Find 5 × 400.

5 × 4 = 20

5 × 40 = 5 × 4 tens
     = 20 tens
     = 200
So, 5 × 40 = 200.

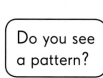

×	4	40	400
5	20	200	2,000

5 × 400 = 5 × 4 hundreds
     = 20 hundreds
     = 2,000
So, 5 × 400 = 2,000.

Do you see a pattern?

Guided Practice

Multiply. Find the missing numbers.

5 Find 6 × 70.

6 × 70 = 6 × [ ] tens

   = [ ] tens

   = [ ]

So, 6 × 70 = [ ].

6 Find 6 × 700.

6 × 700 = 6 × [ ] hundreds

   = [ ] hundreds

   = [ ]

So, 6 × 700 = [ ].

Multiply. Use mental math.

7 8 × 60 = [ ]

8 9 × 400 = [ ]

8 × 6 = [ ]
So, 8 × 60 = [ ].

9 × 4 = [ ]
So, 9 × 400 = [ ].

9   7 × 50 = [ ]

10   90 × 6 = [ ]

11   5 × 70 = [ ]

12   8 × 100 = [ ]

13   600 × 4 = [ ]

14   9 × 800 = [ ]

Let's Practice

Multiply. Use mental math.

1   7 × 6 = [ ]

2   9 × 8 = [ ]

3   4 × 80 = [ ]

4   70 × 3 = [ ]

5   6 × 40 = [ ]

6   20 × 9 = [ ]

7   8 × 700 = [ ]

8   900 × 5 = [ ]

9   7 × 600 = [ ]

10   400 × 2 = [ ]

Recall
4 × 8
7 × 3
6 × 4
2 × 9
8 × 7
9 × 5
7 × 6
4 × 2

ON YOUR OWN

Go to Workbook A:
Practice 1, page 119–120

7.2 Multiplying Without Regrouping

Lesson Objective

- Multiply ones, tens, and hundreds without regrouping.

Learn **Multiply a 2-digit number without regrouping using base-ten blocks.**

$3 \times 12 = ?$

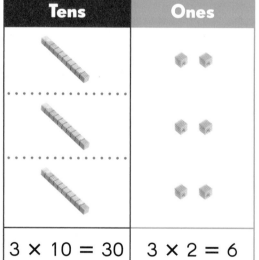

Tens	Ones

Step 1
Multiply the **ones** by 3.

$$\begin{array}{r} 1\ 2 \\ \times\quad 3 \\ \hline \mathbf{6} \end{array}$$

3×2 ones $= 6$ ones

Step 2
Multiply the **tens** by 3.

$$\begin{array}{r} 1\ 2 \\ \times\quad 3 \\ \hline \mathbf{3}\ 6 \end{array}$$

3×1 ten $= 3$ tens

Tens	Ones
$3 \times 10 = 30$	$3 \times 2 = 6$

So, $3 \times 12 = 36$.

36 is the **product** of 3 and 12.

Learn

Multiply a 3-digit number without regrouping using base-ten blocks.

$2 \times 341 = ?$

Hundreds	Tens	Ones
		▫
		▫

Step 1
Multiply the **ones** by 2.

$$\begin{array}{r} 3\ 4\ 1 \\ \times\qquad 2 \\ \hline \mathbf{2} \end{array}$$

2×1 one $= 2$ ones

Hundreds	Tens	Ones
	▬▬▬▬	▫
	▬▬▬▬	▫

Step 2
Multiply the **tens** by 2.

$$\begin{array}{r} 3\ 4\ 1 \\ \times\qquad 2 \\ \hline \mathbf{8}\ 2 \end{array}$$

2×4 tens $= 8$ tens

Hundreds	Tens	Ones
▨▨▨	▬▬▬▬	▫
▨▨▨	▬▬▬▬	▫
$2 \times 300 = 600$	$2 \times 40 = 80$	$2 \times 1 = 2$

Step 3
Multiply the **hundreds** by 2.

$$\begin{array}{r} 3\ 4\ 1 \\ \times\qquad 2 \\ \hline \mathbf{6}\ 8\ 2 \end{array}$$

2×3 hundreds $= 6$ hundreds

So, $2 \times 341 = 682$.

682 is the product of 2 and 341.

Guided Practice

Find the missing numbers.

1 2 × 34 = ?

Step 1   Multiply the ones by 2.

2 × 4 ones = [   ] ones

$$\begin{array}{r} 3\ 4 \\ \times\quad 2 \\ \hline \end{array}$$

Step 2   Multiply the tens by 2.

2 × 3 tens = [   ] tens

So, 2 × 34 = [   ].

$$\begin{array}{r} 3\ 4 \\ \times\quad 2 \\ \hline \end{array}$$

2 3 × 132 = ?

Step 1   Multiply the ones by 3.

3 × [   ] ones = [   ] ones

$$\begin{array}{r} 1\ 3\ 2 \\ \times\quad\ 3 \\ \hline \end{array}$$

Step 2   Multiply the tens by 3.

3 × [   ] tens = [   ] tens

$$\begin{array}{r} 1\ 3\ 2 \\ \times\quad\ 3 \\ \hline \end{array}$$

Step 3   Multiply the hundreds by 3.

3 × [   ] hundred = [   ] hundreds

So, 3 × 132 = [   ].

$$\begin{array}{r} 1\ 3\ 2 \\ \times\quad\ 3 \\ \hline \end{array}$$

Multiply.

3
$$\begin{array}{r} 2\ 4 \\ \times\ 2 \\ \hline \end{array}$$

4
$$\begin{array}{r} 4\ 0 \\ \times\ 2 \\ \hline \end{array}$$

5
$$\begin{array}{r} 2\ 3\ 2 \\ \times\quad 3 \\ \hline \end{array}$$

6
$$\begin{array}{r} 1\ 1\ 2 \\ \times\quad 4 \\ \hline \end{array}$$

Hands-On Activity

WORKING TOGETHER

STEP 1 Each member of the group takes an activity sheet.

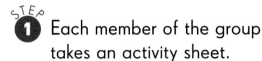

Activity Sheet A		
H	T	O
2	2	1
×		

STEP 2 Group member selects a multiplier card.

STEP 3 Group member places the multiplier card on the ones place on his or her activity sheet. Then he or she finds the product of the number on the activity sheet and the number on the card. The other group members check the answer.

Activity Sheet A		
H	T	O
2	2	1
×		3

STEP 4 The group members take turns to complete their worksheets. Each player completes 2 worksheets.

Let's Practice

Find the missing numbers.

1 3 × 32 = ?

3 × 2 ones = [ ] ones

3 × 3 tens = [ ] tens

So, 3 × 32 = [ ] .

Multiply the ones.
Then multiply the tens.

2 2 × 214 = ?

2 × [ ] ones = [ ] ones

2 × [ ] ten = [ ] tens

2 × [ ] hundreds = [ ] hundreds

So, 2 × 214 = [ ] .

Multiply the ones.
Then multiply the
tens, followed by
the hundreds.

Multiply.

3
```
   2 3
×    2
```
[ ]

4
```
   1 1
×    3
```
[ ]

5
```
   4 2 1
×      2
```
[ ]

6
```
   2 1 3
×      3
```
[ ]

ON YOUR OWN

Go to Workbook A:
Practice 2, page 121–126

7.3 Multiplying Ones, Tens, and Hundreds with Regrouping

Lesson Objective

- Multiply ones, tens, and hundreds with regrouping.

Learn **Multiply a 2-digit number with regrouping of ones.**

$5 \times 15 = ?$

Hundreds	Tens	Ones
		• • • • •

Step 1

Multiply the **ones** by 5.

$$\begin{array}{r} \overset{2}{1}\,5 \\ \times\ \ \ 5 \\ \hline 5 \end{array}$$

5×5 ones $= 25$ ones

Hundreds	Tens	Ones
	⫽	• • • • •

Regroup the ones.
25 ones $=$ 2 tens 5 ones

Hundreds	Tens	Ones
	⫽⫽⫽⫽⫽⫽⫽	• • • • •

Step 2

Multiply the **tens** by 5.

$$\begin{array}{r} \overset{2}{1}\,5 \\ \times\ \ \ 5 \\ \hline 7\,5 \end{array}$$

5×1 ten $= 5$ tens

Add the tens.
2 tens $+$ 5 tens $=$ 7 tens

So, $5 \times 15 = 75$.

Multiply a 2-digit number with regrouping of tens.

$4 \times 31 = ?$

Hundreds	Tens	Ones
		● ● ● ●

Step 1
Multiply the **ones** by 4.

$$\begin{array}{r} 3\ 1 \\ \times\qquad 4 \\ \hline \mathbf{4} \end{array}$$

4×1 one $= 4$ ones

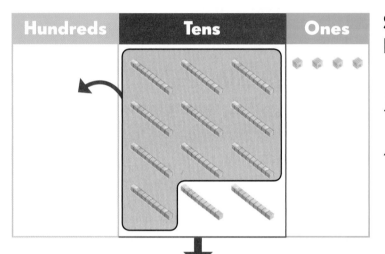

Step 2
Multiply the **tens** by 4.

$$\begin{array}{r} 3\ 1 \\ \times\qquad 4 \\ \hline \mathbf{12}\,4 \end{array}$$

4×3 tens $= 12$ tens

Regroup the tens.
12 tens = 1 hundred 2 tens

So, $4 \times 31 = 124$.

Guided Practice

Find the missing numbers.

1 5 × 12 = ?

Step 1 Multiply the ones by 5.

5 × ⬜ ones = ⬜ ones

$$\begin{array}{r} \square \\ 1\ 2 \\ \times\ \ \ 5 \\ \hline \square \end{array}$$

Regroup the ones.

⬜ ones = ⬜ ten ⬜ ones

Step 2 Multiply the tens by 5.

5 × ⬜ ten = ⬜ tens

$$\begin{array}{r} \square \\ 1\ 2 \\ \times\ \ \ 5 \\ \hline \square \end{array}$$

Add the tens.

⬜ ten + ⬜ tens = ⬜ tens.

So, 5 × 12 = ⬜ .

2
$$\begin{array}{r} 2\ 3 \\ \times\ \ \ 4 \\ \hline \square \end{array}$$

3
$$\begin{array}{r} 4\ 9 \\ \times\ \ \ 2 \\ \hline \square \end{array}$$

4
$$\begin{array}{r} 1\ 7 \\ \times\ \ \ 3 \\ \hline \square \end{array}$$

Find the missing numbers.

5 40 × 3 = ?

Step 1 Multiply the ones by 3.

3 × ⬜ ones = ⬜ ones

$$\begin{array}{r} 4\ 0 \\ \times\ \ \ 3 \\ \hline \square \end{array}$$

Step 2 Multiply the tens by 3.

3 × ⬜ tens = ⬜ tens

$$\begin{array}{r} 4\ 0 \\ \times\ \ \ 3 \\ \hline \square \end{array}$$

Regroup the tens.

⬜ tens = ⬜ hundred ⬜ tens

So, 40 × 3 = ⬜ .

6 37
× 3
_____
[　　]

7 60
× 5
_____
[　　]

8 81
× 4
_____
[　　]

Multiply a 2-digit number with regrouping of ones and tens.

2 × 68 = ?

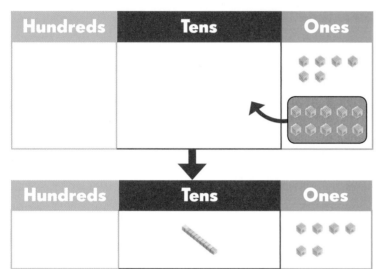

Step 1
Multiply the **ones** by 2.

$$\begin{array}{r} \overset{1}{6}8 \\ \times\ \ \ 2 \\ \hline 6 \end{array}$$

2 × 8 ones = 16 ones

Regroup the ones.
16 ones = 1 ten 6 ones

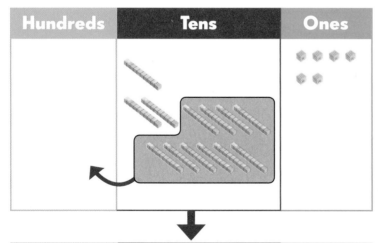

Step 2
Multiply the **tens** by 2.

$$\begin{array}{r} \overset{1}{6}8 \\ \times\ \ \ 2 \\ \hline \mathbf{13}6 \end{array}$$

2 × 6 tens = 12 tens

Add the tens.
1 ten + 12 tens = 13 tens

Regroup the tens.
13 tens = 1 hundred 3 tens

So, 2 × 68 = 136.

Guided Practice

Find the missing numbers.

9 $2 \times 69 = ?$

Step 1 Multiply the ones by 2.

2×9 ones = [ ] ones

Regroup the ones.

[ ] ones = [ ] ten [ ] ones

$$\begin{array}{r} \boxed{} \\ 6\,9 \\ \times \quad 2 \\ \hline \boxed{} \end{array}$$

Step 2 Multiply the tens by 2.

2×6 tens = [ ] tens

Add the tens.

[ ] ten + [ ] tens = [ ] tens

Regroup the tens.

[ ] tens = [ ] hundred [ ] tens

$$\begin{array}{r} \boxed{} \\ 6\,9 \\ \times \quad 2 \\ \hline \boxed{} \end{array}$$

So, $2 \times 69 =$ [ ].

Multiply.

10
$$\begin{array}{r} 9\,3 \\ \times \quad 5 \\ \hline \end{array}$$

11
$$\begin{array}{r} 2\,4 \\ \times \quad 5 \\ \hline \end{array}$$

12
$$\begin{array}{r} 7\,6 \\ \times \quad 2 \\ \hline \end{array}$$

13
$$\begin{array}{r} 8\,8 \\ \times \quad 2 \\ \hline \end{array}$$

14
$$\begin{array}{r} 5\,8 \\ \times \quad 4 \\ \hline \end{array}$$

15
$$\begin{array}{r} 4\,8 \\ \times \quad 3 \\ \hline \end{array}$$

Multiply a 3-digit number with regrouping of ones, tens, and hundreds.

$5 \times 146 = ?$

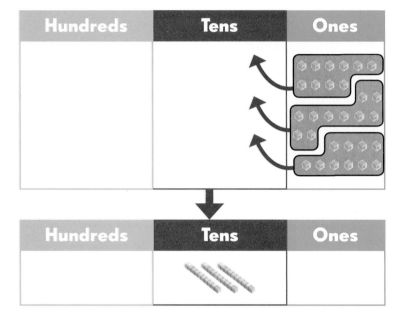

Step 1
Multiply the **ones** by 5.

$$\begin{array}{r} \overset{3}{1\,4\,6} \\ \times 5 \\ \hline \mathbf{0} \end{array}$$

5×6 ones $= 30$ ones

Regroup the ones.
30 ones $= 3$ tens 0 ones

Step 2
Multiply the **tens** by 5.

$$\begin{array}{r} \overset{2}{}\overset{3}{1}\,4\,6 \\ \times 5 \\ \hline \mathbf{3}\,0 \end{array}$$

5×4 tens $= 20$ tens

Add the tens.
3 tens $+$ 20 tens $= 23$ tens

Regroup the tens.
23 tens $= 2$ hundreds 3 tens

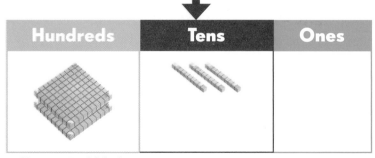

Hundreds	Tens	Ones

Step 3

Multiply the **hundreds** by 5.

$$\begin{array}{r} {}^{2}{}^{3} \\ 1\ 4\ 6 \\ \times 5 \\ \hline \mathbf{7}3\ 0 \end{array}$$

5×1 hundred $= 5$ hundreds

Add the hundreds.

2 hundreds $+$ 5 hundreds
$= 7$ hundreds

So, $5 \times 146 = 730$.

Guided Practice

Find the missing numbers.

16 $4 \times 157 = ?$

Step 1 Multiply the ones by 4.

$4 \times$ ⬜ ones $=$ ⬜ ones

Regroup the ones.

⬜ ones $=$ ⬜ tens ⬜ ones

$$\begin{array}{r} \square \\ 1\ 5\ 7 \\ \times 4 \\ \hline \square \end{array}$$

Step 2 Multiply the tens by 4.

$4 \times$ ⬜ tens $=$ ⬜ tens

Add the tens.

⬜ tens $+$ ⬜ tens $=$ ⬜ tens

$$\begin{array}{r} \square\ \square \\ 1\ 5\ 7 \\ \times 4 \\ \hline \square \end{array}$$

Regroup the tens.

⬜ tens $=$ ⬜ hundreds ⬜ tens

Step 3 Multiply the hundreds by 4.

4 × ▢ hundred = ▢ hundreds

$$\begin{array}{r} 157 \\ \times\ \ \ 4 \\ \hline \end{array}$$

Add the hundreds.

▢ hundreds + ▢ hundreds = ▢ hundreds

So, 4 × 157 = ▢ .

Multiply.

17
$$\begin{array}{r} 395 \\ \times\ \ \ \ 2 \\ \hline \end{array}$$

18
$$\begin{array}{r} 278 \\ \times\ \ \ \ 3 \\ \hline \end{array}$$

19
$$\begin{array}{r} 168 \\ \times\ \ \ \ 5 \\ \hline \end{array}$$

20
$$\begin{array}{r} 247 \\ \times\ \ \ \ 4 \\ \hline \end{array}$$

21
$$\begin{array}{r} 170 \\ \times\ \ \ \ 3 \\ \hline \end{array}$$

22
$$\begin{array}{r} 369 \\ \times\ \ \ \ 2 \\ \hline \end{array}$$

Spin and Multiply!

Players: 2 to 4
Materials:
- transparent spinner base
- 1 spinner with numbers 2, 3, 4, and 5
- game cards 1 to 4

 STEP 1 Player 1 picks a game card.

STEP 2 Player 1 turns the spinner to get a number.

STEP 3 Player 1 writes the number in the box on the game card. He or she multiplies the numbers. The other players check the answer.

STEP 4 The players take turns finding products until each game card is full.

The player with the most correct answers wins!

Let's Practice

Find the missing numbers.

1 3 × 58 = ?

Step 1 Multiply the ones by 3.

3 × 8 ones = [ ] ones

Regroup the ones.

[ ] ones = [ ] tens [ ] ones

```
    [ ]
    5 8
  ×   3
    [ ]
```

Step 2 Multiply the tens by 3.

3 × 5 tens = [ ] tens

Add the tens.

[ ] tens + [ ] tens = [ ] tens

```
    [ ]
    5 8
  ×   3
    [ ]
```

Regroup the tens.

[ ] tens = [ ] hundred [ ] tens

So, 3 × 58 = [ ].

2 5 × 147 = ?

Step 1 Multiply the ones by 5.

5 × 7 ones = ▢ ones

$$\begin{array}{r} 1\ 4\ 7 \\ \times \qquad 5 \\ \hline \end{array}$$

Regroup the ones.

▢ ones = ▢ tens ▢ ones

Step 2 Multiply the tens by 5.

5 × 4 tens = ▢ tens

$$\begin{array}{r} 1\ 4\ 7 \\ \times \qquad 5 \\ \hline \end{array}$$

Add the tens.

▢ tens + ▢ tens = ▢ tens

Regroup the tens.

▢ tens = ▢ hundreds ▢ tens

Step 3 Multiply the hundreds by 5.

5 × 1 hundred = ▢ hundreds

$$\begin{array}{r} 1\ 4\ 7 \\ \times \qquad 5 \\ \hline \end{array}$$

Add the hundreds.

▢ hundreds + ▢ hundreds = ▢ hundreds

So, 5 × 147 = ▢ .

3
$$\begin{array}{r} 2\ 4 \\ \times \quad 3 \\ \hline \end{array}$$

4
$$\begin{array}{r} 5\ 2 \\ \times \quad 4 \\ \hline \end{array}$$

5
$$\begin{array}{r} 5\ 5 \\ \times \quad 2 \\ \hline \end{array}$$

6
$$\begin{array}{r} 1\ 1\ 4 \\ \times \qquad 5 \\ \hline \end{array}$$

7
$$\begin{array}{r} 2\ 8\ 2 \\ \times \qquad 3 \\ \hline \end{array}$$

8
$$\begin{array}{r} 3\ 8\ 7 \\ \times \qquad 2 \\ \hline \end{array}$$

ON YOUR OWN

Go to Workbook A:
Practice 3 and 4, pages 127–137

Put On Your Thinking Cap!

STEP 1 Here are eight number cards.

Find pairs of numbers that add to make 10.

a How many pairs of 10 do you get?

b Sum of the eight numbers = ⬜ × 10

= ⬜

STEP 2 Without adding the numbers one by one, find the sum of numbers 2 to 9.

Find pairs of numbers that give the same sum.

ON YOUR OWN

**Go to Workbook A:
Put on Your Thinking Cap!
pages 139–140**

Chapter Wrap Up

Study Guide

You have learned...

BIG IDEAS

▶ Mental math can be used to multiply.
▶ Numbers up to 3-digits can be multiplied with or without regrouping.

Multiplication

Mental Multiplication Strategies

$4 \times 6 = 24$
So, $6 \times 4 = 24$.
4×6 is the same as 6×4.

$7 \times 30 = 7 \times 3$ tens
$\qquad = 21$ tens
$\qquad = 210$
So, $7 \times 30 = 210$.

$7 \times 300 = 7 \times 3$ hundreds
$\qquad\quad = 21$ hundreds
$\qquad\quad = 2,100$
So, $7 \times 300 = 2,100$.

Multiplication Without Regrouping

$$\begin{array}{r} 3\,4 \\ \times \quad 2 \\ \hline 6\,8 \end{array} \qquad \begin{array}{r} 2\,0\,3 \\ \times \quad\ 3 \\ \hline 6\,0\,9 \end{array}$$

Multiplication with Regrouping

$$\begin{array}{r} {\scriptstyle 3} \\ 7\,8 \\ \times \quad 4 \\ \hline 3\,1\,2 \end{array} \qquad \begin{array}{r} {\scriptstyle 1\ 1} \\ 4\,5\,6 \\ \times \quad\ 2 \\ \hline 9\,1\,2 \end{array}$$

Chapter Review/Test

Vocabulary
Choose the correct word.

product
regroup
multiply

1 When you [____] 4 tens by 3, you get 12 tens.

2 When you [____] 12 tens, you get 1 hundred and 2 tens.

3 When you multiply numbers, the answer is the [____].

Concepts and Skills
Find the missing numbers.

4 6 × 5 = 30
So, 5 × 6 = [____]

5 8 × 40 = 8 × [____] tens

= [____] tens

= [____]

6 9 × 200 = [____] × [____] hundreds

= [____] hundreds

= [____]

Multiply.

7
```
   1 2
×    4
─────────
[____]
```

8
```
   4 8
×    2
─────────
[____]
```

9
```
   7 1
×    2
─────────
[____]
```

10
```
   8 8
×    5
─────────
[____]
```

11
```
  1 3 4
×     2
```

12
```
  3 0 3
×     2
```

13
```
  1 2 4
×     3
```

14
```
  2 0 3
×     4
```

15
```
    8 3
×     3
```

16
```
  2 6 1
×     3
```

17
```
  2 9 7
×     3
```

18
```
  2 3 6
×     4
```

Problem Solving

Solve.

19 Martin has 43 tricycles. How many wheels do the tricycles have in all?

20 There are 4 theaters. Each theater has 249 seats. How many seats are there in all?

Division

Try making 2 equal groups with:

1 6 8 10 12 or 14 children.

2 5 7 9 11 or 13 children.

What do you notice when you try to make 2 equal groups with odd numbers?

BIG IDEA

▶ There can be remainders when dividing to make equal groups or when sharing equally.

Recall Prior Knowledge

Dividing to share equally

Divide 12 into 3 equal groups.
How many does each group have?

$12 \div 3 = 4$

Each group has 4 cubes.

Dividing to form equal groups

Divide 12 equally so that there are 3 in each group.
How many groups are there?

$12 \div 3 = 4$

There are 4 groups.

Division as repeated subtraction

Find $10 \div 2$.

$10 \underbrace{- 2 - 2 - 2 - 2 - 2}_{\text{Subtract groups of two 5 times}} = 0$

So, $10 \div 2 = 5$.

✔ Quick Check

Solve.

1 Divide 15 pencils into 3 equal groups.
   How many pencils does each group have?

2 Jane has 8 apples. She eats 2 apples each day.
   How many days will it take for her to eat all the apples?

Divide. Use repeated subtraction.

3 $12 \div 2 =$

Mental Division

Lesson Objectives

• Use related multiplication facts to divide.
• Use patterns to divide multiples of 10 and 100.

Learn **Use related multiplication facts to help you divide mentally.**

Find 24 ÷ 6.

4 × 6 = 24

So, 24 ÷ 6 = 4.

> Think of a related multiplication fact.

Guided Practice

Divide. Use related multiplication facts to help you.

1 35 ÷ 7 =

> Think of the multiplication facts for 7.

2 63 ÷ 9 =

> Think of the multiplication facts for 9.
>
> × 9 = 63

Use related multiplication facts and patterns to divide mentally.

Find 80 ÷ 4.

Find 800 ÷ 4.

80 ÷ 4 = 8 tens ÷ 4

        = 2 tens

        = 20

So, 80 ÷ 4 = 20.

800 ÷ 4 = 8 hundreds ÷ 4

         = 2 hundreds

         = 200

So, 800 ÷ 4 = 200.

÷	8	80	800
4	2	20	200

Use the multiplication facts for 4.

2 × 4 = 8

8 ÷ 4 = 2

Guided Practice

Find the missing numbers.
Use related multiplication facts and patterns to help you.

3   42 ÷ 6 = ?

420 ÷ 6 = ?

42 ÷ 6 = ☐ ones ÷ 6

      = ☐ ones

      = ☐

So, 42 ÷ 6 = ☐

420 ÷ 6 = ☐ tens ÷ 6

       = ☐ tens

       = ☐

So, 420 ÷ 6 = ☐

Think of the multiplication facts for 6.

☐ × 6 = 42

Let's Practice

Divide mentally. Use multiplication facts for 6 to help you.

1 $30 \div 6 =$ ☐   **2** $24 \div 6 =$ ☐   **3** $54 \div 6 =$ ☐

Divide mentally. Use multiplication facts for 7 to help you.

4 $21 \div 7 =$ ☐   **5** $42 \div 7 =$ ☐   **6** $56 \div 7 =$ ☐

Divide mentally. Use related multiplication facts and patterns to help you.

7 Find $300 \div 3$.

$$300 \div 3 = \boxed{} \text{ hundreds} \div 3$$
$$= \boxed{} \text{ hundred}$$
$$= \boxed{}$$

So, $300 \div 3 = \boxed{}$.

8 Find $350 \div 5$.

$$350 \div 5 = \boxed{} \text{ tens} \div 5$$
$$= \boxed{} \text{ tens}$$
$$= \boxed{}$$

So, $350 \div 5 = \boxed{}$.

9 $700 \div 7 =$ ☐   **10** $560 \div 8 =$ ☐   **11** $360 \div 9 =$ ☐

12 $6,400 \div 8 =$ ☐   **13** $7,200 \div 9 =$ ☐   **14** $2,800 \div 7 =$ ☐

ON YOUR OWN

Go to Workbook A:
Practice 1, pages 147–148

Lesson 8.2 Quotient and Remainder

Lesson Objective

- Divide a 1-digit or a 2-digit number by a 1-digit number with or without a remainder.

Vocabulary
quotient
remainder

Learn Dividing equally.

2 children share 8 pails equally.

a How many pails does each child have?

8 ÷ 2 = ?

8 ones ÷ 2 = 4 ones with no ones left over

quotient = 4 ones

b Each child has 4 pails.

How many pails are left over?

There are no pails left over.

2 × **4** = 8

A **quotient** is the answer to a division problem.
In the division fact 8 ÷ 2 = 4, the quotient is 4.

^{Le}arn **Dividing with remainder.**

4 children share 11 seashells equally.

a How many seashells does each child have?

$11 \div 4 = ?$

> Divide the 11 seashells into 4 equal groups.

11 ones $\div$ 4 = 2 ones with
                       3 ones, left over
              = 2 R 3

> $4 \times \mathbf{2} = 8$
> 8 is less than 11.
> $4 \times \mathbf{3} = 12$
> 12 is more than 11.
> Choose 2 as the quotient.

quotient = 2 ones
remainder = 3 ones

Each child has 2 seashells.

b How many seashells are left over?

3 seashells are left over.

> $11 \div 4 = 2 R 3$
> R3 means there are 3 seashells left over. It also means that there is a **remainder** of 3 seashells.

A **remainder** is the number left over from a division problem.

Guided Practice

Solve.

1 3 friends share 17 starfish equally.

   a How many starfish does each friend have?

     17 ÷ 3 = ?

17 − ▢ − ▢ − ▢ = ▢ Subtract groups of ▢ 3 times. ▢ starfish are left over.	3 × **5** = 15 15 is less than 17. 3 × **6** = 18 18 is more than 17. Choose 5 as the quotient.

17 ones ÷ 3 = 5 ones with 2 ones left over

               = ▢ R ▢

Quotient   = ▢ ones

Remainder   = ▢ ones

17 ÷ 3   = ▢ R ▢

Each friend has ▢ starfish.

   b How many starfish are left over?

     ▢ starfish are left over.

Find the Remainder!

Players: 2 to 4
Materials:
- pasta pieces
- number cards from 10 to 35
- spinner with numbers 3, 4, and 5

STEP 1 Mix up the number cards. Player 1 turns over a card.

STEP 3 Spin the spinner.

STEP 5 Your score is the remainder you get. The other players check the answer using division.

STEP 2 Player 1 takes the number of pasta pieces shown on the card. For example, for the number card 32, take 32 pasta pieces.

STEP 4 Divide the pasta pieces by the number shown on the spinner, and find the remainder.
For example, if Player 1 spins a 5:
- he rearranges the 32 pasta pieces into 5 equal groups, and
- counts the pieces in each group, and the remaining pieces.

The quotient is 6.
The remainder is 2.

STEP 6 Players take turns to play two rounds each.

The player with the most points wins!

Guided Practice

Find the missing numbers.

2 20 ones ÷ 3 = [ ] R [ ]

Quotient = [ ] ones

Remainder = [ ] ones

3 43 ones ÷ 5 = [ ] R [ ]

Quotient = [ ] ones

Remainder = [ ] ones

Let's Practice

Find the missing numbers.

1 16 ones ÷ 4 = [ ]

Quotient = [ ] ones

Remainder = [ ] ones

2 15 ones ÷ 2 = [ ] R [ ]

Quotient = [ ] ones

Remainder = [ ] one

Think of the multiplication facts for 2.

6 × 2 = [ ]

7 × 2 = [ ]

8 × 2 = [ ]

Choose [ ] as the quotient.

3 41 ÷ 5 = [ ] R [ ]

4 33 ÷ 4 = [ ] R [ ]

5 29 ÷ 3 = [ ] R [ ]

ON YOUR OWN

Go to Workbook A:
Practice 2, pages 149–150

8.3 Odd and Even Numbers

Lesson Objective

- Use different strategies to identify odd and even numbers.

Learn Use building blocks to identify odd and even numbers.

Use 1, 3, 5, 7, and 9 building blocks to make this pattern.

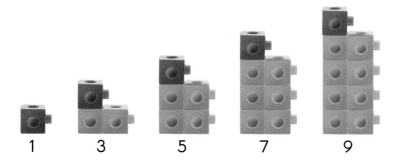

| 1 | 3 | 5 | 7 | 9 |

These numbers are odd numbers.

> **Odd numbers** have 1, 3, 5, 7, or 9 in the ones place.

Name some odd numbers.

Make patterns using 2, 4, 6, 8, and 10 building blocks.

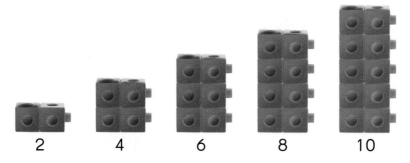

| 2 | 4 | 6 | 8 | 10 |

These numbers are even numbers. 0 is also an even number.

> **Even numbers** have 2, 4, 6, 8, or 0 in the ones place.

Name some even numbers.

Divide by 2 to identify odd numbers.

Look at this group of odd numbers.

ODD
13 17 19

Divide each number by 2.

Example

6 × 2 = 12. 12 is less than 13.
7 × 2 = 14. 14 is more than 13.
Choose 6 as the quotient.

What do you notice?

$$13 - 2 - 2 - 2$$
$$- 2 - 2 - 2 = 1$$
There is a remainder.

> When an odd number is divided by 2, there is always a remainder of 1.

Guided Practice

Divide.

1 11 ÷ 2 =   **2** 15 ÷ 2 =

Divide by 2 to identify even numbers.

Look at this group of even numbers.

EVEN
12 16 20

Divide each number by 2.

Example

6 × 2 = 12

$$12 - 2 - 2 - 2$$
$$- 2 - 2 - 2 = 0$$
There is no remainder

What do you notice?

> When an even number is divided by 2, there is no remainder.

Guided Practice

Solve.

3 Look at the numbers below. Decide whether each number is odd or even without dividing.

8　**17**　**26**　**38**　**77**　**129**

Explain your answers.

Let's Practice

Solve.

1 Is 23 an even number? Explain your answer.

Divide each number by 2.
Then decide if the number is odd or even.

2 21 ÷ 2 =

21 is a   number.

3 18 ÷ 2 =

18 is a   number.

ON YOUR OWN

Go to Workbook A:
Practice 3, pages 151–152

Division Without Remainder and Regrouping

Lesson Objective

- Use base-ten blocks and place value to divide 2-digit numbers without regrouping or remainders.

Use partial products to divide.

3 friends share 63 squashes equally.
How many squashes does each friend get?
$63 \div 3 = ?$

Tens	Ones

Step 1

Divide the **tens** by 3.

6 tens ÷ 3 = 2 tens

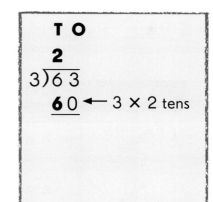

```
   T O
    2
3)6 3
  6 0  ← 3 × 2 tens
```

Step 2

Divide the **ones** by 3.

3 ones ÷ 3 = 1 one

So, $63 \div 3 = 21$.

```
    2 1  ← Quotient
3)6 3
  6 0
  ───
    3
    3  ← 3 × 1 one
    0  ← Remainder
```

Each friend gets 21 squashes.

Guided Practice

Solve.

1 3 friends share 39 tomatoes equally.
How many tomatoes does each friend get?

$39 \div 3 = ?$

Tens	Ones

Step 1

Divide the **tens** by 3.

$3 \text{ tens} \div 3 = $ [blank] ten

$$\begin{array}{r} \text{T O} \\ 1 \\ 3\overline{)3\ 9} \\ 3\ 0 \end{array}$$

Tens	Ones

Step 2

Divide the **ones** by 3.

$9 \text{ ones} \div 3$
$= $ [blank] ones

So, $39 \div 3$
$= $ [blank].

Each friend gets

[blank] tomatoes.

$$\begin{array}{r} 1\ \mathbf{3} \\ 3\overline{)3\ 9} \\ 3\ 0 \\ \hline 9 \\ \mathbf{9} \\ \hline \mathbf{0} \end{array}$$

Divide. Use base-ten blocks to help you.

2 48 ÷ 2 = ?

Step 1   Divide the tens.

⬜ tens ÷ 2 = ⬜ tens

Step 2   Divide the ones.

⬜ ones ÷ ⬜ = ⬜ ones

So, 48 ÷ 2 = ⬜

3 Find 69 ÷ 3 = ?

Step 1   Divide the tens.

⬜ tens ÷ ⬜ = ⬜ tens

Step 2   Divide the ones.

⬜ ones ÷ ⬜ = ⬜ ones

So, 69 ÷ 3 = ⬜

Divide. Use base-ten blocks to help you.

4

4)4 8

5

5)5 5

6

2)6 4

7

3)9 0

8

4)8 4

9

3)6 6

Let's Practice

Divide. Use base-ten blocks to help you.

1 9 ones ÷ 3 = ☐ ones   **2** 5 tens ÷ 5 = ☐ tens

3 8 tens ÷ 4 = ☐ tens   **4** 6 ones ÷ 2 = ☐ ones

Divide. Use base-ten blocks to help you.

5 96 ÷ 3 = ?

Divide the tens.

9 tens ÷ 3 = ☐ tens.

Divide the ones.

6 ones ÷ 3 = ☐ ones

So, 96 ÷ 3 = ☐ .

Divide. Use base-ten blocks to help you.

6 ☐ ☐
   3)9   6

7 ☐ ☐
   2)8   2

8 ☐ ☐
   4)4   8

9 ☐ ☐
   5)5   0

Solve.

10 Rebecca buys 44 tennis balls.
She packs the tennis balls equally into 4 bags.
How many tennis balls does Rebecca pack into each bag?

11 Fernando has 84 marbles.
He divides the marbles equally into 2 groups.
How many marbles are there in each group?

ON YOUR OWN

**Go to Workbook A:
Practice 4, pages 153–154**

Division with Regrouping in Tens and Ones

Lesson Objective

- Use base-ten blocks and place value to divide a 2-digit number by a 1-digit number with regrouping, with or without remainders.

Regroup to divide.

Jason and Brad collect rocks. They share 32 rocks equally.
How many rocks does each boy get?

$32 \div 2 = ?$

Tens	Ones

Step 1

Divide the **tens** by 2.

3 tens ÷ 2
= 1 ten with
1 ten left over

```
    T O
    1
2)3 2
    2 0  ← 2 × 1 ten
    1
```

Tens	Ones

Regroup the
1 ten left over.
1 ten = 10 ones

Add the ones.
10 ones + 2 ones
= 12 ones

```
    1
2)3 2
    2 0
    1 2
```

Tens	Ones

Step 2

Divide the **ones** by 2.
12 ones ÷ 2 = 6 ones

```
    1 6
2)3 2
    2 0
    1 2
    1 2  ← 2 × 6 ones
      0
```

So, $32 \div 2 = 16$.
Each boy gets 16 rocks.

Guided Practice

Solve.

1 3 friends share 56 trading cards equally.
How many cards does each boy get?
How many cards are left over?

$56 \div 3 = ?$

Step 1

Divide the **tens** by 3.
5 tens ÷ 3

= [ ] ten with

remainder [ ] tens

Regroup the remainder tens.
2 tens = 20 ones
Add the ones.
20 ones + 6 ones
= 26 ones

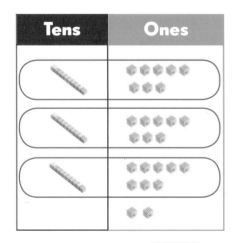

Step 2

Divide the **ones** by 3.

[ ] ones ÷ 3

= [ ] ones with

remainder [ ] ones

So, 56 ÷ 3
= [ ] R [ ] .

Each friend gets [ ] cards.

[ ] cards are left over.

```
T O
  1
3)5 6
  3 0   ← 3 × 1 ten
  2
```

```
  1
3)5 6
  3 0
  2 6
```

```
  1 8 R 2
3)5 6
  3 0
  2 6
  2 4   ← 3 × 8 ones
  2
```

Hands-On Activity

WORK IN PAIRS

Materials:
• base-ten blocks

Use base-ten blocks to help you divide!

Regroup each remainder ten into 10 ones.

a Divide 7 tens 2 ones between 2 children.

b Divide 5 tens and 7 ones into 3 baskets.

c Divide 9 tens and 6 ones among 4 families.

Guided Practice

Divide. Use base-ten blocks to help you.

2 $4\overline{)5\ 6}$

3 $5\overline{)7\ 5}$

4 $2\overline{)7\ 9}$

Solve. Use base-ten blocks to help you.

5 Mr. Ross divides 63 books into stacks of 5.

a How many stacks are there?

b How many books are left over?

Let's Practice

Divide.

1 18 ones ÷ 2 = [ ] ones

2 18 ones ÷ 3 = [ ] ones

3 15 ones ÷ 3 = [ ] ones

4 15 ones ÷ 5 = [ ] ones

Find the missing numbers.

5 96 = 8 tens [ ] ones

6 54 = [ ] tens 24 ones

Divide. Give the remainder in tens. Use base-ten blocks to help you.

7 5 tens ÷ 2 = [ ] tens with remainder [ ] ten

8 8 tens ÷ 3 = [ ] tens with remainder [ ] tens

Divide. Give the remainder in ones. Use base-ten blocks to help you.

9 5 tens ÷ 3 = [ ] ten with remainder [ ] ones

10 7 tens ÷ 4 = [ ] ten with remainder [ ] ones

Divide.

11
2)3 4

12
3)5 1

Solve.

13 Timothy packs 60 bottles of orange juice equally into 4 coolers.
How many bottles are in each cooler?

ON YOUR OWN

Go to Workbook A:
Practice 5, pages 155–156

PROBLEM SOLVING

Find the missing numbers.

1

```
      4  5
  2) 9  ▢
     8  0
     1  0
     1  0
        0
```

2

```
     ▢▢  ▢▢
  5) 7  ▢
     5  0
     2  6
     2  5
        1
```

3

```
      1  7
  ▢) 6  ▢
     4  0
     2  ▢
    ▢▢  ▢▢
        1
```

4

```
     ▢▢  ▢▢
  ▢) 9  ▢
     6  0
     3  0
        ▢▢
        0
```

ON YOUR OWN

**Go to Workbook A:
Put on Your Thinking Cap!**
pages 157–158

Chapter Wrap Up

Study Guide
You have learned...

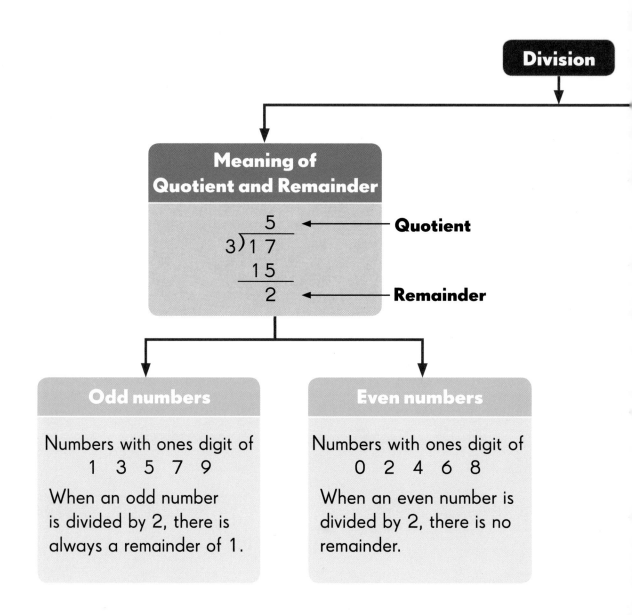

Division

Meaning of Quotient and Remainder

$$3\overline{)17}$$ quotient 5, 15, remainder 2

Quotient

Remainder

Odd numbers

Numbers with ones digit of
1 3 5 7 9

When an odd number is divided by 2, there is always a remainder of 1.

Even numbers

Numbers with ones digit of
0 2 4 6 8

When an even number is divided by 2, there is no remainder.

BIG IDEA

▶ There can be remainders when dividing to make equal groups or when sharing equally.

Divide

Mentally by recalling multiplication facts	**A 2-digit number by a 1-digit number (no regrouping)**	**A 2-digit number by a 1-digit number (with regrouping)**
Find $90 \div 3$. $90 \div 3 = 9$ tens $\div\ 3$ $\qquad\ = 3$ tens $\qquad\ = 30$ So, $90 \div 3 = 30$. Find $900 \div 3$. $900 \div 3 = 9$ hundreds $\div\ 3$ $\qquad\quad = 3$ hundreds $\qquad\quad = 300$ So, $900 \div 3 = 300$.	$$\begin{array}{r} 1\,2 \\ 4\overline{)4\,8} \\ 4\,0 \\ \hline 8 \\ 8 \\ \hline 0 \end{array}$$ ⟵ 4 × 1 ten ⟵ 4 × 2 ones	$$\begin{array}{r} 2\,5 \\ 3\overline{)7\,5} \\ 6\,0 \\ \hline 1\,5 \\ 1\,5 \\ \hline 0 \end{array}$$ ⟵ 3 × 2 tens ⟵ 3 × 5 ones

Chapter Review/Test

Vocabulary
Choose the correct word.

even
remainder
odd
quotient

1 The answer in a division problem is called a _____ .

2 When an _____ number is divided by 2, there is always a _____ of 1.

3 When an _____ number is divided by 2, there is no remainder.

Concepts and Skills
Find the missing numbers.

4 _____ × 5 = 30

30 ÷ 5 = _____

5 _____ × 3 = 21

21 ÷ 3 = _____

6 _____ × 4 = 36

36 ÷ 4 = _____

Divide. Use related multiplication facts to help you.

7 54 ÷ 6 = _____   6 × _____ = 54

540 ÷ 6 = _____

5,400 ÷ 6 = _____

8 35 ÷ 7 = _____   7 × _____ = 35

350 ÷ 7 = _____

3,500 ÷ 7 = _____

Divide.

9 $44 \div 4 =$

10 $86 \div 2 =$

11 $93 \div 3 =$

12 $38 \div 2 =$

13 $54 \div 3 =$

14 $72 \div 4 =$

15 $65 \div 5 =$

16 $43 \div 3 =$

17 $59 \div 4 =$

18 $99 \div 5 =$

Problem Solving

19 A farmer has 36 sheep. He has 4 sheep pens.
He keeps an equal number of sheep in each pen.
How many sheep does each pen have?

20 Lisa bakes 45 muffins.
She puts the muffins equally into 3 boxes.
How many muffins are in each box?

21 Sharon needs 69 plastic butterflies for her mobiles.
She puts 4 plastic butterflies on each mobile.
a How many mobiles does she have?
b How many butterflies are left over?

22 Paul has 58 bicycles in his shop.
He arranges them in 5 equal rows.
a How many bicycles are in each row?
b How many bicycles are left over?

Using Bar Models: Multiplication and Division

How many children are on the red mats? How many children are on yellow mats?

Lessons

9.1 Real-World Problems: Multiplication

9.2 Real-World Problems: Two-step Problems with Multiplication

9.3 Real-World Problems: Division

9.4 Real-World Problems: Two-step Problems with Division

BIG IDEA

▶ Bar models can be used to solve different kinds of multiplication and division word problems.

Recall Prior Knowledge

Using bar models to solve multiplication problems

Multiply 3 by 4.

$4 \times 3 = 12$

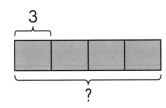

Using bar models to solve division problems

1 Divide 24 by 3.

$24 \div 3 = 8$

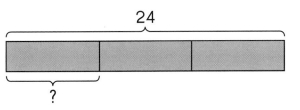

2 Divide 14 into groups of 2.

$14 \div 2 = 7$

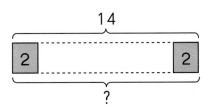

✔ Quick Check

Complete each multiplication sentence. Use bar models to help you.

1

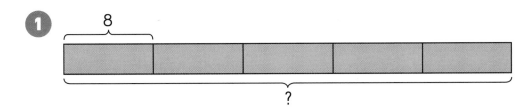

_____ × _____ = _____

Complete each multiplication sentence. Use bar models to help you.

2

$$\boxed{} \times \boxed{} = \boxed{}$$

Complete each division sentence. Use bar models to help you.

3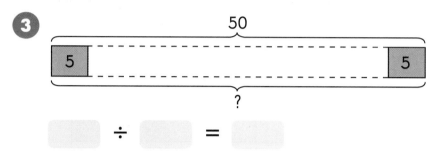

$$\boxed{} \div \boxed{} = \boxed{}$$

4

28

?

$$\boxed{} \div \boxed{} = \boxed{}$$

Draw bar models.

5 4 × 9 = ?

6 56 ÷ 8 = ?

Real-World Problems: Multiplication

Lesson Objective

Vocabulary
twice

- Use bar models to solve one-step multiplication word problems.

Learn **Use bar models to solve one-step multiplication word problems.**

There are 5 boxes of pencils.
Each box contains 12 pencils.
How many pencils are there in all?

12 pencils

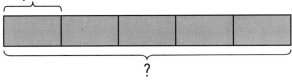

?

1 unit ⟶ 12

5 units ⟶ 12 × 5 = 60

There are 60 pencils in all.

Guided Practice

Solve. Use a bar model to help you.

1. Mark pays $195 a month for rent.
   How much rent does he pay in all for 3 months?

$195

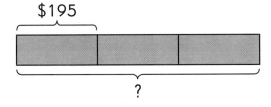

?

1 unit ⟶ $ [   ]

3 units ⟶ $ [   ] × [   ] = $ [   ]

He pays $ [   ] in all for 3 months.

Learn **Use bar models to solve one-step multiplication word problems.**

Zach has 342 stamps.
Ron has **twice** as many stamps as Zach.
How many stamps does Ron have?

342 stamps

Zach

Ron

?

$342 \times 2 = 684$

Ron has 684 stamps.

Twice is 2 times.

 stands for 342 stamps.

So, stands for 342 stamps × 2.

Guided Practice

Solve. Use bar models to help you.

2 The Garden Center sells 250 packs of seeds. Fran's Nursery sells 3 times as many packs of seeds as the Garden Center. How many packs of seeds does Fran's Nursery sell?

250 packs of seeds

Garden Center

Fran's Nursery

?

☐ × ☐ = ☐

Fran's Nursery sells ☐ packs of seeds.

☐ stands for 250 packs of seeds

So, ☐☐☐ stands for 250 packs of seeds × 3.

Let's Practice

Solve. Draw bar models to help you.

1 On Monday, Mrs. Bollat sells 424 movie tickets.
On Tuesday, she sells twice as many tickets as on Monday.
How many tickets does she sell on Tuesday?

2 A newsstand has 7 boxes of magazines.
Each box contains 120 magazines.
How many magazines does the newsstand have in all?

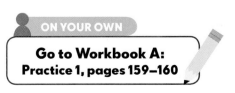

ON YOUR OWN

**Go to Workbook A:
Practice 1, pages 159–160**

Real-World Problems: Two-step Problems with Multiplication

Lesson Objectives

- Use bar models to solve two-step word problems.
- Choose the correct operations to solve two-step word problems.

Learn **Use bar models to solve two-step word problems.**

Gas Station A sells 273 gallons of gas in the morning. On the same morning, Gas Station B sells **double** the amount of gas that Gas Station A sells.

Double means 2 times.

a How many gallons of gas does Gas Station B sell?

b How many gallons of gas do they sell in all?

273 gallons

Gas Station A

Gas Station B

b ?

a ?

a 273 × 2 = 546
Gas Station B sells 546 gallons of gas.

b 273 + 546 = 819
They sell 819 gallons of gas in all.

Guided Practice

Solve. Use bar models to help you.

1 A bookstore had 4 shelves of books.
Each shelf had 116 books.
The store owner sold 382 books.
How many books were left?

> Find the total number of books at first.

116 books

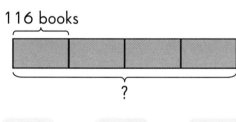

?

[ ] × [ ] = [ ]

There were [ ] books at first.

[ ] books

382 books   ?

[ ] ● [ ] = [ ]

There were [ ] books left.

Solve. Use bar models to help you.

2 Randy has some oranges and apples.
He puts 2 oranges and 3 apples into each box.
He has a total of 6 boxes of fruit.
How many pieces of fruit does Randy have in all?

[　　] + [　　] = [　　]

2 oranges   3 apples

There are [　　] pieces of fruit in each box.

1 box [　　　　　]

[　　] pieces of fruit

[　　] pieces of fruit

[　　　　　　　　　　　]

?

1 unit ⟶ [　　]

6 units ⟶ [　　] × 5 = [　　]

Randy has [　　] pieces of fruit in all.

3 Flo saves 4 times as much money as Larry.
Maria saves $12 less than Flo.
Larry saves $32.
How much money does Maria save?

1 unit ⟶ $[　　]

4 units ⟶ $[　　] × [　　] = $[　　]

Flo saves $[　　].

$[　　] − $[　　] = $[　　]

Maria saves $[　　].

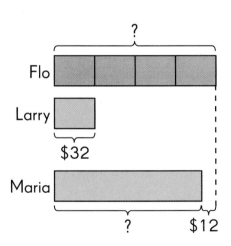

?

Flo

Larry

$32

Maria

? $12

Let's Practice

Decide whether to add, subtract, or multiply at each step.
Then solve the word problem. Use bar models to help you.

1 One bag of peanuts costs $5.
Alicia wants to buy 8 bags of peanuts
but she has only $33.
How much more money does she need?

2 Megan makes a necklace with 12 red beads
and 15 yellow beads.
She makes a total of 3 necklaces.
How many beads does she use in all?

3 Sandy has $60.
She wants to buy 7 teddy bears.
If each teddy bear cost $6, how much
money does she have left?

4 Pat is 12 years old.
James is 3 times as old as Pat.
Raymond is 9 years younger than James.
How old is Raymond?

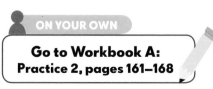

ON YOUR OWN

Go to Workbook A:
Practice 2, pages 161–168

WORKING TOGETHER

Write a two-step word problem using these words and numbers. Then draw bar models and solve it.

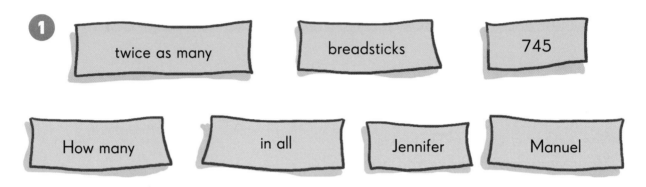

1

twice as many

breadsticks

745

How many

in all

Jennifer

Manuel

These are bar models drawn for another word problem. Write a two-step word problem for the bar models.

2

A

B

C

14

3

9.3 Real-World Problems: Division

Lesson Objectives

- Use bar models to solve one-step division word problems.
- Recognize number relationships.

Learn Use bar models to solve one-step division word problems.

A grower picks 60 oranges.
The grower packs them equally into 5 boxes.
How many oranges does the grower pack in each box?

60 oranges

?

$60 \div 5 = 12$

He packs 12 oranges in each box.

Guided Practice

Solve. Use bar models to help you.

1 There are 48 crayons.
They are packed equally into 4 boxes.
How many crayons does each box have?

[   ] ÷ [   ] = [   ]

Each box has [   ] crayons.

48 crayons

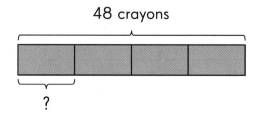

?

Solve. Use bar models to help you.

2 A tricycle has 3 wheels.
In Jerome's shop, the tricycles have 42 wheels in all.
How many tricycles does Jerome have?

42 ÷ [____] = [____]

There are [____] tricycles in Jerome's shop.

42 wheels

| 3 | | 3 |

?

Use bar models to solve one-step division word problems.

Shawn and Trish scored 36 goals in all.
Shawn scored 3 times as many goals as Trish.
How many goals did Trish score?

4 units ———→ 36
1 unit ———→ 36 ÷ 4 = 9

Trish scored 9 goals.

Shawn

Trish

} 36

?

Guided Practice

Solve. Use bar models to help you.

3 Ahmad sells 32 video games.
He sells 4 times as many video games as Justin.
How many video games does Justin sell?

[____] units ———→ [____]

[____] unit ———→ [____] ÷ [____]

= [____]

Justin sells [____] video games.

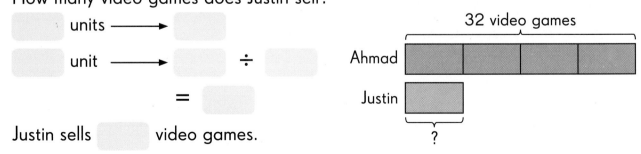

32 video games

Ahmad

Justin

?

Let's Practice

Solve. Draw bar models to help you.

1 Mr. Lee packs 80 pounds of rice into 5-pound bags.
How many bags does he use?

2 During a school fair, Daniel sells 87 cups of juice.
He sells 3 times as many cups of juice as Rodney.
How many cups of juice does Rodney sell?

3 The total age of Melvin and Jack is 72 years.
Melvin is 3 times as old as Jack.
How old is Jack?

4 Darren uses 4 pieces of wood to make 1 picture frame.
How many frames can he make with 72 pieces of wood?

5 A bowling alley has 81 bowling balls.
Each lane has 9 balls beside it.
How many lanes does the bowling alley have?

ON YOUR OWN

**Go to Workbook A:
Practice 3, pages 169–172**

Lesson 9.4 Real-World Problems: Two-step Problems with Division

Lesson Objectives:

- Use bar models to solve two-step word problems.
- Choose the correct operations to solve two-step word problems.

Learn **Use bar models to solve two-step word problems.**

A baker has 28 ounces of flour.
He uses 8 ounces of it to make biscuits.
He packs the remaining flour into 5 equal bags.

a How much flour is left?

b How many ounces of flour does each bag have?

a $28 - 8 = 20$

20 ounces of flour is left.

28 ounces

? | 8 ounces

b $20 \div 5 = 4$

Each bag has 4 ounces of flour.

20 ounces

?

Guided Practice

Solve. Use bar models to help you.

1 Joel buys 3 boxes of pencils. Each box contains 32 pencils.
The pencils are shared equally among 4 children.
How many pencils does each child get?

32 pencils

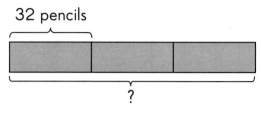

?

First, find out how many
pencils Joel buys.

32 × 3 = ____

Joel buys ____ pencils.

____ pencils

?

Then find out how many
pencils each child get.

96 ÷ 4 = ____

Each child gets ____ pencils.

2 Rodrigo buys 3 boxes of buttons. Each box contains 16 buttons.
He packs the buttons into bags of 8 buttons each.
How many bags of buttons does he have?

____ × ____ = ____

Rodrigo has ____ buttons.

____ ÷ ____ = ____

He has ____ bags of buttons.

16

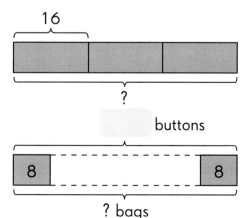

?

____ buttons

8   8

? bags

3 Jackie, Kim, and Minah have 55 stamps in all.
Jackie has twice as many stamps as Kim.
Minah has 10 stamps.
How many stamps does Kim have?

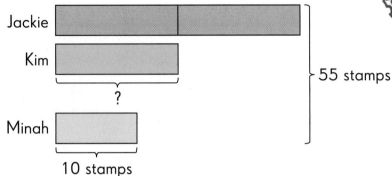

☐ − ☐ = ☐

Jackie and Kim have ☐ stamps.

3 units ⟶ ☐

1 unit ⟶ ☐ ÷ 3 = ☐

Kim has ☐ stamps.

READING AND WRITING MATH
Math Journal

WORKING TOGETHER

Write two-step word problems using these words and numbers. Then solve. Use bar models to help you.

1

| Vincent | breadsticks | shared equally | Tony |

| altogether | 45 | How many | 21 |

These are bar models drawn for another word problem. Write a two-step word problem for the bar models. Then solve it.

2

A

B

C

Let's Practice

Decide whether to add, subtract, multiply, or divide at each step. Then solve the word problem. Use bar models to help you.

1 Joe has 32 envelopes and Pete has 48 envelopes.
They share the envelopes equally.

a How many envelopes do they have in all?

b How many envelopes does each of them have?

2 Naomi has 29 biscuits.
She gives Charlie 9 biscuits.
She divides the rest of the biscuits
among 5 people. How many biscuits
does each person have?

3 Dina, Sue, and Kelley have $98 in all.
Dina has 4 times as much money as Kelley.
Sue has $18.
How much money does Kelley have?

4 Adam, Ben, Carlos, and Darren share a $96 bill for dinner equally.
They each also tip the waitress $2.
How much does each of them spend in all?

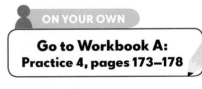

ON YOUR OWN

Go to Workbook A:
Practice 4, pages 173–178

PROBLEM SOLVING

Solve. Use bar models to help you.

1 Mr. King has a total of 19 geese, chickens, and ducks on his farm.
He has 3 more chickens than geese.
He has 2 fewer ducks than geese.
How many ducks does he have?

Use the **bar models** to help you solve the problem.

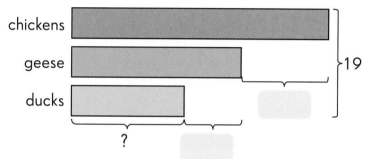

chickens

geese

ducks

19

?

2 Gita puts tires on 21 bicycles and tricycles.
She uses 53 tires in all.
How many tricycles are there?

ON YOUR OWN

**Go to Workbook A:
Put on Your Thinking Cap!
pages 179–180**

Chapter Wrap Up

Study Guide
You have learned...

> **Using Bar Models : Multiplication and Division**

> **One-step**

Multiplication

Chloe has 3 boxes of hairclips.
Each box has 12 hairclips.
How many hairclips does Chloe have in all?

12 hairclips

?

$12 \times 3 = 36$
Chloe has 36 hairclips in all.

Division

Tom has 42 toy soldiers.
He keeps them equally in 3 drawers.
How many toy soldiers are there in each drawer?

42

?

3 units ⟶ 42
1 unit ⟶ $42 \div 3 = 14$
There are 14 toy soldiers in each drawer.

Clark divides 72 stamps equally among the pages of his album.
Each page has 8 stamps.
How many pages of the album has stamps?

72 stamps

? pages

$72 \div 8 = 9$
9 pages of the album has stamps.

BIG IDEA

▶ Bar models can be used to solve different kinds of multiplication and division word problems.

Two-step

Multiplication

Josie has 4 black T-shirts. She has 3 times as many white as black T-shirts. How many T-shirts does she have in all?

$3 \times 4 = 12$

$12 + 4 = 16$

Josie has 16 T-shirts in all.

Division

Elsie divides 20 paper clips equally among 4 girls. She then gives each girl 2 more paper clips. How many paper clips does each girl have?

$20 \div 4 = 5$

$5 + 2 = 7$

Each girl has 7 paper clips.

Multiplication and Division

Douglas has 4 boxes of pencils. Each box has 10 pencils. He gives the pencils to 8 children. How many pencils does each child get?

$40 \div 8 = 5$

Each child gets 5 pencils.

$4 \times 10 = 40$

He has 40 pencils.

Chapter Review/Test

Vocabulary

Choose the correct word.

| divide |
| twice |
| multiply |
| double |

1 When we [____] 5 by 2, we get a product of 10.

2 Two times a number is [____] or [____] that number.

Concepts and Skills

Match each model to a word problem. Then solve the problem.

3   •

4   •

5   •

6 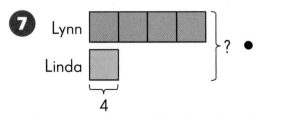   •

7

7 Lynn / Linda   ? •

• Lynn has 4 times as many trading cards as Linda. Linda has 4 trading cards. How many trading cards do they have in all? **A**

• Linda shares 24 trading cards equally among 4 girls. How many trading cards does each girl receive? **B**

• Linda has 6 packs of trading cards. There are 8 trading cards in each pack. How many trading cards are there in all? **C**

• Linda has 24 trading cards. She packs them into 6 packs equally. How many trading cards does each pack have? **D**

• Lynn has 24 trading cards. She gives 4 trading cards each to some girls. How many girls are there? **E**

Problem Solving

Solve.

8 Andrea has 6 vases.
She puts 3 roses and 4 lilies in each vase.
How many flowers are there in all?

9 A carpenter orders 84 doors.
He orders 3 times as many red doors as blue doors.
How many blue doors does he order?

10 Tim has 8 pieces of wood.
He saws each piece into 5 smaller pieces.
He then packs them equally into 4 bundles.
How many pieces of wood does each bundle have?

11 There are 51 children at a party.
A clown brings some balloons to the party.
He bursts 15 balloons while trying to inflate them.
How many balloons does he bring if each child receives 3 balloons?

Glossary

- **area model of multiplication**

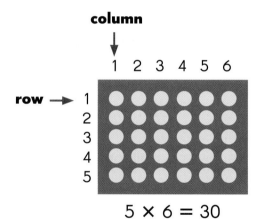

$$4 \times 7 = 28$$

- **array model of multiplication**

An arrangement in rows and columns.

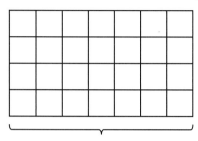

$$5 \times 6 = 30$$

- **Associative Property of Multiplication**

Changing the way numbers in a multiplication sentence are grouped and multiplied does not change the answer.

$$3 \times 2 \times 5 = 6 \times 5$$
$$= 30$$
$$3 \times 2 \times 5 = 3 \times 10$$
$$= 30$$

B

- **bar model**

  The bar model helps to solve word problems. Bars are drawn, labelled with all the relevant information, and divided according to the situation in the word problem.

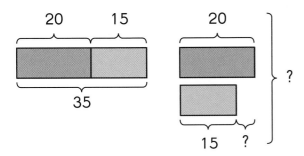

C

- **Commutative Property of Multiplication**

  Changing the order of numbers in a multiplication sentence does not change the answer.
  10 × 2 = 20
  2 × 10 = 20

D

- **difference**

  The difference is the answer to a subtraction problem.
  1,047 − 23 = 1,024,
  1,024 is the difference between 1,047 and 23.

- **digit**

  A number is made up of digits.
  In the number 1,479, the digits are 1, 4, 7, and 9.

- **division**

  This is an operation of making equal groups. It is used to find the number of groups, or the number in each group.

- **dot paper**

  A dot paper shows a set of dots in equal rows and equal columns. It is an example of an array.

- **double**

  2 times

- **equal groups**

  These are equal groups.
  They both have the same number of items.

- **estimate**

  An estimate is a number close to the exact number.
  396 is 400 when rounded to the nearest hundred.
  400 is an estimate.

- **even number**

  Any number that has the digit 0, 2, 4, 6, or 8 in its ones place is an even number. 12, 354, 7,956 are even numbers.

- **expanded form**

  The expanded form of a number shows the value of each digit in it. 2,000 + 400 + 70 + 5 is the expanded form of 2,475.

F

- **front-end estimation**

  Front-end estimation uses leading digits to estimate sums and differences.

G

- **greater than (>)**

  Use *greater than* when comparing two numbers.

  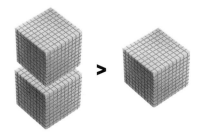

  2,000 **>** 1,000
  2,000 is greater than 1,000.

- **greatest**

  Use *greatest* when comparing more than two numbers.

  2   200   2,000

  2,000 is the greatest number.

L ───────

- **leading digit**

  The leading digit in a number is the digit with the greatest place value. The leading digit for **2**,475 is **2**.

- **least**

  Use *least* when comparing more than two numbers.

  2   200   2,000

  2 is the least number.

- **less than (<)**

  Use *less than* when comparing two numbers.

  1,000 < 2,000
  1,000 is less than 2,000.

M ───────

- **multiplication**

  This is an operation of repeated addition. It can be shown by using area, array, and number line models.

- **Multiplicative Property of One**

  Any number multiplied by 1 equals that number.

  $2 \times 1 = 2 \qquad 7 \times 1 = 7$

- **Multiplicative Property of Zero**

  Any number multiplied by 0 equals 0.

  $3 \times 0 = 0 \qquad 7 \times 0 = 0$

N

- **number line**

  1,734 1,834 1,934 2,034

O

- **odd number**

  Any number that has the digit 1, 3, 5, 7, or 9 in its ones place is an odd number. 11, 203 and 1,245 are odd numbers.

P ─────

- **place value**

  The value of a digit in a number.
  In 8,769, the digit 8 is in the thousands place.

- **place-value chart**

Thousands	Hundreds	Tens	Ones
8	7	6	9

- **place-value strips**

- **product**

  A product is the answer in a multiplication problem.
  5 × 7 = 35
  35 is the product of 5 and 7.

Q ─────

- **quotient**

  A quotient is the answer to a division problem.
  8 ÷ 2 = 4
  4 is the quotient.

R

- **reasonable**

  1,245 + 2,534 = 3,779

  1,245 rounded to the nearest thousand is 1,000.

  2,534 rounded to the nearest thousand is 3,000.

  The estimated sum is 4,000.

  3,779 is close to 4,000 so the answer is reasonable.

- **regroup**

  To change:

  10 ones to 1 ten or 1 ten to 10 ones;
  10 tens to 1 hundred or 1 hundred to 10 tens;
  10 hundreds to 1 thousand or 1 thousand to 10 hundreds.

- **remainder**

  A remainder is the number left over from a division problem.

  11 ÷ 2 = 5 R 1
  When 11 is divided by 2, the remainder is 1.

- **rounded**

  Term used in estimating numbers to the nearest ten or hundred.

  2,476 is 2,480 when rounded to the nearest ten.

  2,436 is 2,400 when rounded to the nearest hundred.

  2,456 is 2,500 when rounded to the nearest hundred.

- **rule**

  To find the missing number in the number pattern, the rule is to either add 100 to the number before it or subtract 100 from the number after it.

S

- **skip**

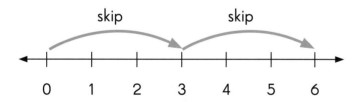

  2 skips of 3 show 2 groups of 3.

- **standard form**

  2,478 is the standard form of 2,478.

- **sum**

  The sum is the answer to an addition problem.
  123 + 45 = 168
  168 is the sum of 123 and 45.

T

- **ten thousand**

  1 more than 9,999 is 10,000.

- **twice**

  2 times

V

- **value**

  In 2,475,
  the value of the digit 2 is 2,000
  the value of the digit 4 is 400
  the value of the digit 7 is 70
  the value of the digit 5 is 5.

W

- **word form**

  Two thousand, four hundred seventy-eight is the word form of 2,478.

Index

Pages listed in black type refer to Pupil Book A.
Pages in blue type refer to Pupil Book B.
Pages in *black italic* type refer to Workbook (WB) A pages.
Pages in *blue italic* type refer to Workbook (WB) B pages.
Pages in **boldface** type show where a term is introduced.

Pages listed in black type refer to Pupil Book A.
Pages in blue type refer to Pupil Book B.
Pages in *black italic* type refer to Workbook (WB) A pages.
Pages in *blue italic* type refer to Workbook (WB) B pages.
Pages in **boldface** type show where a term is introduced.

Pages listed in black type refer to Pupil Book A.
Pages in blue type refer to Pupil Book B.
Pages in *black italic* type refer to Workbook (WB) A pages.
Pages in *blue italic* type refer to Workbook (WB) B pages.
Pages in **boldface** type show where a term is introduced.

Photo Credits

Blank

$$4 + 5 = 9$$
$$6 + 4 = 10$$